TALES FROM THE OPEN ROAD

The Adventures and Misadventures of RV Living

****

By Joe Russo
We're the Russos

Copyright © 2019 by We're the Russos, LLC

All rights reserved.

No part of this book may be reproduced in any form or by any electronic or mechanical means, including information storage and retrieval systems, without written permission from the author, except for the use of brief quotations in a book review.

DEDICATION

To Kait.
Without you and your crazy ideas, none of this would have been possible.

PROLOGUE

"Take risks and have a lot of children."

This is one of the last things my father told me before he passed away in 2013. By then, Kait and I had been together for eight years and our idea of taking a risk entailed not checking our work emails at night. We had what many would consider a great life. A house in the suburbs of Los Angeles, two dogs, five motorcycles, a couple cars in the driveway and well-paying careers.

While things looked great on paper, neither of us were happy with our work nor our lives. We began to realize that our time was no longer our own. We'd become slaves to the system—being told what time to be at work each day, when we could leave and to be available even when we weren't in the office. Each of us spent about three hours a day commuting to and from the office. The little time we did have together at night was spent decompressing in front of the TV. Weekends were never long enough and we dreaded heading back into the office Monday morning. We knew we had to make a change. Then on Mother's Day, 2014, our lives changed forever.

We'd headed to Kait's parents' house to spend the day with her mom. Kait had been under a lot of stress due to work and was hoping to spend an uninterrupted day enjoying her parents' company, but that wasn't to be the case. Shortly after we arrived, she began getting messages from work that required her immediate attention. It was the straw that broke the camel's back. She'd finally had enough and said, "I can't do this anymore! We should just quit our jobs, sell the house and buy an RV. We can travel around the country with our dogs, Duke and Leo, and enjoy life now!" Initially I thought Kait was joking, but when she told me she was serious, I called her crazy. Give up our house and jobs to travel around in a RV without an income? No way.

Shortly thereafter, I had to leave to go spend time with my mother and on the way out, Kait made me promise to at least think about the idea. On the drive to my mother's house, I did just that. Yes, the idea was crazy, but I began thinking back to those last words from my father: "Take risks." If ever there was a risk I was going to take, this would be it. I called Kait and said, "Let's do it!"

Within a few weeks, we had a plan in place and began shopping for the perfect motorhome. Our goal was to leave toward the end of the year but fate had other plans for us. I got an offer from work that would keep me there another year. As much as I wanted to hit the road, this would put us in a much better spot financially and allow us more time to plan our adventure. The idea was to save enough to allow us to travel the country for a year. During that time, we'd look for a new place to settle and when we were ready, we'd put down stakes again and go back to work.

As it turns out, having that extra time came in handy. The search for the motorhome seemed endless. Every time we would zero in on something, another model or type of RV would turn us in another direction. We looked at just about every type of RV on the market until we finally found the one: a brand new Newmar Bay Star 2903. At just under thirty feet, it was smaller than most of the other motorhomes we were considering, but we loved the layout. When we first walked in, we knew it was the one and made an offer that day.

In parallel to our RV shopping, we were also getting our home ready to sell and starting the long process of downsizing our lives from a 1,250 square-foot house to a motorhome. Kait had no problem letting go of things. It seemed that after every load of stuff she dropped off at the donation center, she'd come back even happier than when she left. I on the other hand had difficulty letting go. In the end though, there was only so much room in the motorhome and, aside from a few keepsakes we left with our parents, we weren't getting a storage unit. If it didn't fit in the motorhome, we got rid of it.

At the end of August 2015, the house had sold and we had put in our notices at work. It wasn't easy getting to that point. Along the way I had my doubts as to whether we were doing the right thing. It scared me to think that I would be giving up my career and a solid paycheck to set off into the unknown. Kait was nervous as well, but she had no doubts about what we were doing. Her strength helped me get through some tough times.

After the house sold, we took the motorhome and parked it in front of my mother's house. The plan was to finish up our last week of work and then take a second week to get any last minute preparations done before hitting the road. Once we had everything done and packed in the motorhome, we said goodbye to my mother and that's where this story picks up.

If you're interested in reading all about our journey to get to this point, check out the first book in this series, <u>Take Risks: One Couple's Journey to Quit Their Jobs and Hit the Open Road</u> at https://weretherussos.com/books/ Enjoy!

1. FIRST DAY ON THE ROAD

Sunday, September 13th, 2015

Day 1

With everything loaded, we get our dogs, Duke and Leo, into our new twenty-nine foot Class A motorhome and attach the Jeep to the back. After we run through a pre-departure checklist, we are ready for the open road. My heart begins racing as I put the motorhome in drive. So much has been building up to this very moment.

"You know," I say, looking over at Kait as I take my foot off the brake and begin driving down the street, "we did it. So many people said we wouldn't get here, but we actually did it. Regardless of what happens now, no one can take that away from us, even if we go up in a ball of flames."

Kait's smile goes from ear to ear and she says, "This thing better not go up in flames, otherwise I want a refund!"

A short drive later through the streets of the San Fernando Valley in California, we pull onto the US 101 freeway heading north to our first destination on this year long journey to freedom.

Sitting at a vineyard in Paso Robles, California I lift up my glass to Kait and say, "To our first day on the road."

Completely content, she just smiles and clinks her glass of wine against mine. The sun is going down over the vineyard creating an absolutely gorgeous sunset. Duke and Leo are asleep next to us, and I still can't believe we made it.

"This is what I imagined when we decided to do this!" Kait exclaims, breaking her silence. "We're staying on a vineyard, in California, drinking wine, watching the sunset, and Duke and Leo are here to enjoy it with us. Pura vida!"

"Plus," I respond with a smile, "there's nothing better than doing a tasting, buying a bottle and not having to worry about driving home since ours is parked right here."

"I'm very happy we learned about Harvest Hosts. I have a feeling we're going to be doing this a lot more in the next year."

When we pulled up this afternoon in our motorhome, the owner of the vineyard, Carol, had us park in the dirt lot behind the tasting room. Once we were settled, she came over to give us a quick tour of the property. Just outside of the tasting room, there is a large grass area surrounded by the vineyard that they use for weddings. Across from where we parked, a small garden stood at the edge of the hill, past which we saw rolling hills with endless rows of grapevines.

As Kait and I stood taking this all in, Carol said, "The vineyard is yours, so feel free to explore and pick anything you want from the garden." We felt right at home.

"Do you want to take a walk around the vineyard?" Kait asks, as I sip the last of the wine in my glass.

"I'm pretty happy here at the moment but I think the boys would love to go exploring, so I'm up for it if they are."

Duke seems to understand and immediately sits up and puts a giant paw in my lap. "I guess that answers that question," I say with a laugh.

The vineyard is beautiful. The world around us seems to disappear as we get deeper into the rows of vines. I begin to feel like I'm putting my previous life behind me. It becomes a religious experience, but rather than washing away sins, I'm cleansing myself of a life that was toxic to my soul. Trading material possessions for experiences. Experiences that will help me grow as a person and give me something to look forward to each morning, rather than the dread I used to feel every time the alarm went off.

After our walk, we pack up our folding camp chairs and stuff them back into the rear bay of our motorhome. At twenty-nine feet, the Newmar Bay Star 2903 is smaller than most Class A motorhomes and with less storage space, we—actually that should read, *I*—had to cram as much stuff as I could in the bays. I put emphasis on the "I" because the more Kait seems to get rid of, the happier she is. Downsizing from a 1,250 square foot home was difficult for me, but I was able to fit everything I wanted to bring and then some. Kait doesn't think we'll use half of it but my philosophy is that it's better to have it and not need it, than need it and not have it.

Once we're back inside, Kait asks if I'd like her to make something for dinner. I'm still full from our lunch and all the pretzels we had during the wine tasting so I decide to skip dinner and relax for the rest of the evening. Crawling into bed with my Kindle, I can't stop thinking about this day. The culmination of everything we went through for the last year and a half. Our first day on the road, we can say we took a risk and we made it happen.

That's not to say I wasn't a nervous wreck this morning. We'd spent the last week at my mom's house in Los Angeles, living out of the motorhome with it parked on the street. We needed a place to "crash" after selling the house and still had a few final preparations to get done.

It was nice to have a garage to use while we finished getting our Jeep Wrangler ready to tow, among other things. I was so focused on what needed to get done, I didn't take time to think that we were just days away from leaving until I woke up this morning.

"Holy shit, we're jobless and our 'home' is on wheels," was my first thought. Granted it's a nice motorhome, but it's not what most Americans would consider a permanent residence. In fact, some might even go so far as to call us homeless.

Kait had gotten up about an hour earlier and was cool as a cucumber when I walked into my mom's house from the motorhome and saw her. Her demeanor was so calming that I was relaxed by the time I poured my first cup of coffee. My mom, however, was a total wreck, just as I had been. The fact that we were leaving today and would be gone for at least a year also seemed to hit her this morning. She gave us both a teary goodbye and told us she was headed to the beach because she couldn't stand to watch us leave.

After that, the first hour on Highway 101 North was a blur until I looked down at our rearview monitor to check the Jeep in tow. "Is the brake cable that runs from the tow bar to the Jeep fraying?" I asked.

Kait got up and went to check the cable from the rear window and confirmed that the plastic coating on the cable had been worn off, but it didn't look like the cable underneath had been affected. She asked if I wanted to head back to my mother's so we could fix it, but I wasn't about to turn around after only an hour. Although I was being stubborn about turning back, I did share her concern.

The tow bar that connects the Jeep to the motorhome has a built in mechanical braking system. The cable in question is attached to a second, shorter cable on the Jeep which is attached to the brake pedal. The other end of the cable is attached to a small arm on the tow bar. When the brakes are applied in the motorhome, the force of the Jeep pushing against the tow bar causes the small arm to pull the cable and apply the brakes to the Jeep. We liked the idea of this inertia-based system because there are no electronics to malfunction. It never occurred to me that we would have a problem with the cables.

I justified not turning around by telling myself this wouldn't be the last issue we'd run into and we needed to learn how to deal with this kind of problem on the road. Worst case, we could detach the Jeep and drive separately until we replaced the cable. I brought more than enough tools to fix most problems, so I wasn't worried, just annoyed that we hadn't made it through the first day without having an issue.

There aren't any rest areas around the Ventura or Santa Barbara areas so we decided to keep going and stop at the rest area in Gaviota to check the cable. As we pulled in, the lot was much smaller than either of us had remembered. There are only a handful of spots big enough to fit a large truck or motorhome towing a car. A semi truck was parked in one and cars parked in the rest. We remarked that the cars should be parked in the standard spots, but no one seemed to care. When nature calls, you take the first spot available.

With no space to park the motorhome, we drove through the rest area and got back on Highway 101. I wasn't too worried about the brake cable, but I did have to go to the bathroom after all the coffee I drank. As we drove, I continued looking for a place to pull over so I could use the bathroom in the motorhome. Every pull-out I saw was either too short or too narrow for us to stop safely.

Eventually as we came up and over a hill, there was a large shoulder to pull over. Although we were on the downhill side, I figured this would be fine for a quick bathroom break for me and the boys. "Are you sure we should stop here?" Kait asked with a nervous look.

"It will be fine," I said as a semi truck barreled past us down the hill and the motorhome swayed from the wind. "Well, maybe not."

Despite the situation, my body wasn't going to wait any longer. I jumped out of the seat and ran back to the bathroom. Each truck that passed felt like it was going faster than the last and I had to brace against the wall to stay steady. Kait was afraid to go out with the boys, so once I was done, I took them out for a quick break, then dragged them back inside.

"Let's not do that again," Kait said once we were safely back on the highway.

I learned an important lesson. Don't assume that you'll always have a place to park a large motorhome. It seems like common sense, but I realized that we both need to get into the mindset that we're driving a 20,000 pound vehicle that's over fifty feet long with the Jeep in tow. While I understood its larger size, I never stopped to think about how to handle situations like the one we'd just experienced.

Unfortunately, with the rush to get out of that situation, I'd forgotten to take a look at the fraying cable. I could still see that it was attached in the rearview camera, so I decided that we could take a look at it the next time we stopped. With an average of 6-8 MPG and only half a tank left, it wouldn't be long before we'd need to fill-up, so I had Kait find a gas station along our route.

An hour later we pulled into a Costco for gas. Our motorhome has an eighty-gallon gas tank and the sixty-gallon fill-up took almost fifteen minutes. The nice thing about the two pumps Costco has in each lane is that I was able to pull the motorhome far enough forward to use the first pump to fill it and the second to fill the Jeep.

While I was waiting for the motorhome to fill, I checked the cable. Upon examination I noticed that the black plastic coating on the cable had been worn off where it feeds through a guide hole. The problem was that I had installed the cable off center where it goes into the Jeep. When the cable was pulled, it rubbed against the guide hole. Checking the exposed steel cable, I noticed that the aircraft-grade steel cable was intact and not fraying, which gave me a sense of relief that we'd at least make it to our first destination.

Just before 4 p.m., we pulled up to the vineyard and a huge sense of relief washed over me. With multiple stops and driving at a speed of fifty-five miles per hour, what would typically be a three hour drive became five-and-a-half hours. I didn't realize how wound up I was while we were driving. At one point on the highway, there was construction along the shoulder, causing the lanes to narrow. I was in the right lane and found myself driving along a wall of concrete construction barriers placed along the edge of the lane, giving me no room for error. I'm still trying to get accustomed to keeping the motorhome between the lines, so by the time we made it past the construction, my hands were stark white from how tight I'd been gripping the steering wheel. Kait never said anything, but I knew she was scared to death, probably more so since she was looking right down at those barriers.

After arriving Kait, went in to meet Carol, and I stayed with the boys. When they came out, Carol directed us to park on the backside of the tasting room, along a row of trees, so we had some shade and a sunset view of the hills.

Once parked, I leveled the motorhome using the hydraulic jacks, then extended the slides. Kait asked me to take the boys for a walk while she got everything inside set up. Mainly, she needed us out of the way so she could lay rugs down to cover the laminate flooring. Leo, our white Siberian Husky, has a hard time walking on slippery floors and is much more comfortable walking on the rugs.

Duke and Leo were more excited than I've seen them in a long time. During our walk, they were dragging me around the vineyard, sniffing every inch. It makes me happy to see them so excited and enjoying this new place. If they're like this everywhere we go, it's going to be hard on them to stop traveling once we settle again in a year. I say that because our intention is only to be on the road for a year, and as we travel, look for a place to settle and find new jobs.

"Hey honey, what are you reading?" Kait asks, walking into the bedroom.

"Huh?" I reply, looking down at the blank screen of my Kindle. "Oh, nothing actually. I never even turned it on. I couldn't stop thinking about our day and everything we went through."

"It was quite the day, but we made it and had some delicious wines. Plus the boys seem completely wiped out. Duke and Leo are passed out on their beds. I'm wiped out too, so I'm going to say goodnight."

"Goodnight, honey, and congratulations on our first day on the road." Kait says, sliding under the covers and rolling over. "Oh, and don't forget to call the tow bar company in the morning."

"I won't, and congratulations."

Over a year ago, we decided to take a risk and it seemed like a long shot at the time, but we managed to make our dream of living life on our own terms a reality. Today is the start of our new lives.

BONUS CONTENT: Want to see some video footage from our first few days on the road? Check out this review we did of Harvest Hosts (https://weretherussos.com/harvest-hosts-review/) and, at the very end of the article, is a video featuring the vineyard!

2. DECOMPRESSING

Tuesday, September 15th, 2015

"I'd like to get some work done on our blog," Kait said, as we woke up to another beautiful day on the vineyard.

Shortly before we left Los Angeles, Kait and I decided to start a blog. We thought it would be a fun way to document our journey and let our friends and family know what we were up to. We spent a lot of time trying to come up with a name. It seemed like every blogger had some cool name, and we figured we needed one too; however, neither of us could agree on one. One night, out of the blue, Kait came up with it, "We should name our blog after the movie that started it all." And so We're the Russos (weretherussos.com) was born, named after the movie, <u>We're the Millers</u>.

"I'm good with that," I respond. "Why don't we find a coffee shop? It should be nice out, so the boys can sit outside with us, I can get some coffee, and you can use their Wi-Fi to work on the site."

When we don't have Wi-Fi, we have the ability to use our phone's data plan and tether to computers to get on the Internet, but we only have ten gigabytes of data each month. Posting articles on our website shouldn't take up much data, but if we watch YouTube videos or try to stream shows on Netflix, those ten gigs can go quickly. Places like coffee shops are going to become a valuable resource for us because for a cup or two of coffee, we can use their Wi-Fi for as long as we'd like. Many campgrounds offer Wi-Fi, but we don't plan on spending much time at them. Plus, we've heard the Internet speed at most parks is only good enough to check email.

"Do you think we could make any money off our blog?" I ask.

"I don't know. I want our site to be a resource for people where we share the places we camp, things we do and maybe even our monthly expenses. We can try to monetize it with ads, but we don't have any traffic to the site yet. I think we should start posting a couple articles a week, and once we start seeing a decent amount of views on our site, we can try to monetize it."

"Good point. Who knows? Maybe one day we'll make enough to pay for our coffees."

"Don't you mean *your* coffee? I'm drinking tea," Kait says, as she gives me one of her smiles. "You have a problem, you know that?"

"Coffee isn't a problem; it's a solution!"

Kait spends the next few hours writing an article for the site and getting all of our social platforms set up. When we bought the domain name for our website, we also signed up for all of the corresponding "We're the Russos" accounts on Facebook, Instagram, Twitter and Pinterest. We weren't sure if we would use them all but figured it was better to have them and not use them than not have them. We also have a YouTube channel, but after Kait tried filming me on our last day of work, we decided video wasn't in our future. Neither of us are comfortable with a camera being stuck in our face and decided to put all our efforts towards our website.

"Can I ask you a favor?" Kait asks, looking slightly annoyed as I'm busy surfing the net.

"What's that?"

"You're the designer in the family. Can you create the banners and images for all of our social platforms?"

"Now?"

"Well, it'd be nice to have them sometime today."

"Oh. I wasn't planning on doing any work for a while. We just quit our jobs, and I need some time off to relax and recover before I jump into something else."

"How much time do you think you'll need?"

"I was thinking a couple weeks. The last thing I want to do right now is any type of work."

"I understand. I need to decompress too, but if we want the website to be successful, we need to get started on it and put the time in. Otherwise, what's the point?"

"True," I say with a laugh.

"What's so funny?"

"Well, we've spent the last year talking about how we couldn't wait to quit our jobs and get on the road to just relax and enjoy ourselves, and we don't even make it three days before you jump right back into it."

Kait looks a bit taken aback. She's been working since she was sixteen, and I don't think she quite knows how to step away. I see where she is coming from, though. Since we only saved enough to keep us on the road for a year, any money we make could potentially keep us on the road that much longer, or at least help us to not use up all of our savings.

Before Kait is able to respond, I say, "If you really think we could make some money on this, I'm willing to help. I just need some time before I can dive in."

"That's fine. I can get the site rolling, but I still need some help with the graphics. It shouldn't take too long, and once I have them I won't bug you for a while."

"Okay, I can probably knock those images out pretty quickly and then get back to doing nothing."

I graduated from college with a degree in computer graphics. The idea was that after graduation I would go to work designing video games. As luck would have it, when I graduated in 2002, the market for video games had crashed and companies were struggling to keep their doors open. Not the best climate to be looking for your first real job. For a few years, I worked as a freelancer in various positions before being recruited by my last company, where I stayed for ten years. Although I've never really used my degree, Kait still calls me her "designer." Although I'm a bit rusty, I still know what I'm doing.

I have the graphics to Kait in about twenty minutes and go back to reading endless discussions on the different forums I follow. It's a completely mindless activity and just what I need right now. Like I told Kait, I need some time to decompress. I've had the same routine for the last ten years, and it's hard to sit here and not think about my former projects at work. I actually panicked for a second this morning when I realized it's Tuesday and I hadn't prepped anything for the weekly status meeting. Despite the fact that I realized I no longer had to worry about the meeting, it didn't stop my heart from racing for a few moments. Although I've stepped away from that lifestyle, it's going to take some time before I can put it behind me.

"Are you okay, honey?" Kait asks looking up from her computer.

I didn't realize it, but I've been sitting here rubbing my temples for the last few minutes.

"I think I'm getting a migraine."

What I don't tell Kait is that I'm getting stressed out. I'd hoped to not have to worry about anything for a year. No work, no projects...nothing. Now Kait's expecting me to put time into our website which, and this is the most stressful part, has me thinking about going back to work full-time in a year. The only reason I haven't said no to Kait's plan is the idea that we might be able to delay the end of this trip.

"Let me finish up this post, and we can get you back to the motorhome," she says.

Over the last ten years, migraines have become a constant companion. About eight months after I started at the company, I began having multiple migraines per week. It took me years to realize they were related to the stress I was experiencing at work. My hope has been that once we hit the road, I'll be [relatively] stress free and the migraines might stop, but that seems far from reality right now.

Back at the motorhome, Kait puts together dinner, and I take something for the pain. I feel the meds kicking in and my migraine begin to slip away. Luckily, I caught this one quickly and it isn't too bad, but there have been days that I've held an ice pack to my head and cried.

"You're looking a bit better," Kait says after we finish dinner. "Why don't you go lay down and get a good night's sleep?"

"Good idea. The day is catching up with me, and we have a long day of driving tomorrow."

"We still need to figure out where we're going," Kait says.

"Let's figure it out in the morning," I respond, before crawling into bed.

BONUS CONTENT: Kait and I created a four part series called, Live Life on Your Own Terms where we share our personal experiences and learnings from the five years it took us to transition to this lifestyle: https://weretherussos.com/live-life-on-your-own-terms/

3. THE ROAD TO VEGAS

Wednesday, September 16th, 2015

We knew that when we hit the road we would need to be flexible. We didn't make any plans or reservations. It's always how we've traveled. We only had a general idea of which direction we wanted to head. The idea was that after leaving the vineyard in Paso Robles, we would continue north through California, hugging the coast into Washington and then turn east, staying in the north until the weather got too cold. However, like they say in the military, no plan survives first contact with the enemy. In our case, the enemy was turning out to be Mother Nature.

A few days before we hit the road, fires broke out in Oregon. The last few years have been very dry, so the fires spread quickly. By the time we were ready to continue north, reports were coming in that it was very smoky, and many areas had been closed off. Armed with the new information, we decided to change direction and head toward Fort Collins, Colorado: a 1,200-mile route that will take us through Nevada, a tiny corner of Arizona and Utah. One of my closest friends lives there with his family and with it being one of the best cities for beer, it was an easy decision.

After making some coffee, we begin packing up the motorhome. In the few days we've been at the vineyard, it seems like things have exploded inside. It takes us close to a half hour to put everything away, roll up all the carpets and bring the slides in. Once again we go through our pre-departure checklist, and I go out to double-check the tire pressures and make sure all of the external storage bays are locked.

"It's my turn to drive today!" Kait exclaims, as I walk back inside.

"You sure?" I ask. "The GPS is telling us that it's going to take almost four hours to get to Barstow. That probably means six or seven with stops and everything else."

"I've got this," she responds, sliding into the driver's seat.

It's nine a.m. and I've got the route all set in our RV-specific Garmin. The GPS has a feature that allows me to input all the dimensions and weight of the motorhome so it can guide us around low bridges and routes that have weight restrictions. It also warns us of steep grades and various other hazards along the way. Being new to driving such a large vehicle, it's taken away a lot of the worry we had about driving in unfamiliar areas.

"We need to pick up some food." Kait says as we pull onto the main road. "I saw there was a Costco on our route, I just need to know where to exit."

"Where is it?"

"In Bakersfield. I starred it on the map."

Kait's referring to Google Maps. When we started planning this adventure, we saved all of the places we wanted to see on Google Maps, leaving a star at each location. Now whenever one of us finds a place worth saving, we "star" it. This has left us with a map of the U.S. that looks like a Christmas tree.

"I thought we were only starring places we wanted to see?" I ask.

"I was laying in bed last night when I looked up the Costco and it was just easier to star it than have to look it up again this morning. Now all I have to tell you is to find the star in Bakersfield."

"Huh, good thinking. If we keep this up, we'll be able to track our progress across the country by following the stars."

We both have a good laugh, and about two hours later Kait pulls off the highway for the Costco. The fuel gauge shows two-thirds full, and gas here is cheap, so she pulls into line at the pumps. "If you want to hop in the driver's seat and get us filled up, I'll run inside and pick up a few things," Kait says as she undoes her seat belt.

At the sight of Kait getting up, Duke's ears go up and his tail starts wagging. "Not now, buddy," I say, grabbing his collar so Kait can get out the door without our eighty-pound pup trying to follow her.

We love Costco and have been members for years. When we were getting close to hitting the road, we debated getting rid of our membership because we didn't think we'd have room for bulk items like toilet paper, but I'm glad we kept it. They have a good selection of food and many other things we buy, lower prices on gas than other stations in the area and a great return policy. We also have their credit card which gives us cash back on all our purchases, plus additional cash back on gas, restaurants and travel. The cash back on our fill-ups is more than going to pay for the membership, plus there are a lot of other items in the store that we don't have to buy in bulk.

Moving into the driver's seat, I put the motorhome in drive and move forward with the other cars in front of me.

I look in the side view mirrors and shake my head at the cars lining up behind me. Lucky for them I'm only putting in about twenty-five gallons, but if I were close to empty, they'd be waiting for a good twenty minutes or so.

After I'm done at the pump, I find a spot to park just as Kait comes out of the store. She's pushing a fully-loaded shopping cart and looking very pleased with herself.

"Look what I got!" Kait exclaims holding up a giant bag of potato chips. "I figured we could snack on them during our drive."

"Oh, those look good. What else did you get?"

Kait goes through the basket and the last item she shows me is a six-pack of beer. "They had some microbrews at this Costco, so I thought you might like to try one. Why don't we get everything put away then walk the boys before we get back on the road."

A couple hours and half a bag of potato chips later, we decide to continue past Barstow, CA and keep going to Las Vegas, NV. It's still very hot in Barstow, and there are a few hours of daylight left. If we don't stop again, we should get to Vegas just before sundown. Kait says she's up for it, and I'm enjoying the drive.

"I heard there are some casinos that let you park overnight for free," Kait tells me. "Want to see if you can find one for us?"

"Sure, I'll see what I can find."

I open the AllStays Camp and RV app on my phone and search for Las Vegas. The app displays different RV-related services and campgrounds so I filter the results to only show casinos that allow overnight parking. As I select various casinos, there are notes from fellow RVers about their experience there. So far most of the notes for the casinos I've checked state that they no longer allow overnight RV parking.

One of the byproducts of Vegas' growth over the years is the disappearance of wide open parking lots. Real estate has become too valuable, so tall parking structures have become a part of the skyline to accommodate the ever-growing number of visitors. At 12'8" tall, there isn't a parking structure in town we'd fit in.

"Maybe try one of the casinos off the strip," Kait suggests.

After checking the app and finding a potential place, I call the casino to verify that they still allow overnight parking. I'm told they have an overflow lot where they allow people who are visiting the casino to park their RVs overnight. I certainly don't mind spending a few bucks at the casino if that means we can get a free night of parking. While we could plunk down fifty dollars or more to stay at a campground, we decided to try and do as much free camping as possible. That means staying overnight at casinos, Walmarts and other places that allow it or on federal BLM or Forest Service land. The more free camping we can do, the less we spend which means we can stay on the road for that much longer.

Having lived for so long in Los Angeles, we've both spent our fair share of time in Las Vegas and have no plans to see the sights. It's been in the eighties at night, and we don't want to leave the boys in the motorhome unattended. Our plan is to get a good night's sleep and leave early the next morning to get to Colorado.

Coming down the hill on Interstate 15, we see the casino in the distance. The sun is reflecting off its gold windows, and the GPS announces Kait's upcoming exit.

"Did the person you spoke to tell you where the lot was?" Kait asks.

"Uh, she said it's across from the main lot. I'm sure we'll see it once we make the right off the exit."

Turning onto the main drag in front of the casino, Kait says, "I don't see anything; you?"

"No. Take a right up there and come around the other side of the casino."

As Kait comes around to the back end of the casino, we see a dead end that is too tight for us to u-turn, and we can't back the RV up when the Jeep is in tow.

"What do we do now?" Kait asks, with annoyance in her voice.

"I don't know," I respond in frustration. The long drive has been tiring for the both of us and, aside from the half bag of potato chips, neither of us have had anything resembling a meal.

"Pull up along side this truck," I say pointing to a row of semi trucks. "You get the Jeep detached so we can turn around, and I'll call the casino to figure out where we're supposed to park."

Kait doesn't say anything and silently heads outside to work on getting the Jeep free. Calling the casino again, I'm told we drove right past the lot and to simply go back the way we drove in.

After Kait gets the Jeep detached, I have her follow me over to the lot. Pulling in, I see rows of RVs and semi trucks parked. Most look like they'll be there for the night, and I slip in between two motorhomes. The spots are long enough to accommodate a semi truck and trailer, so we have more than enough room.

Once we're parked, Kait asks if we can put the slides out. Our motorhome has two, one in the bedroom on the passenger side and a full-wall slide on the driver's side. I explain that because the parking spaces are narrow, the slides would extend into the other spots and may block someone or get accidentally hit. We love how the full-wall slide almost doubles the interior room when it's out, but more importantly when it's in, we can still access and use everything inside. When we were shopping, we'd always ask to see the motorhome with the slides in. We saw some where, when the slides were in, you couldn't access the bathroom or bedroom.

Another important feature for us is having the bedroom slide on the passenger or curb side of the motorhome. When we're street camping, this allows us to put the bedroom slide out so it hangs over the curb. With the bedroom slide in, our feet touch the cabinets when we're sleeping, but it's fine for a night or two.

"I think we both need a good meal, let me get dinner started," Kait says, "Do you want to go into the casino?"

"I may as well go make a deposit for our stay. Who knows? I could get lucky!"

"Good luck, honey. I'm going to stay here and relax. That drive took a lot out of me."

Ten minutes later I've already lost what I planned to gamble and remember that old saying, "A fool and his money are soon parted." Grabbing a coffee from the food court, I head back to find a pork and tofu stew simmering on the stove. Kait hands me a bowl, and we both sit in silence while we eat.

"I feel a lot better," I say grabbing one of the beers out of the fridge.

"Me too, I was getting hangry."

"Ha! I love it, 'hangry'. I think we were both hangry. I'm sorry I got frustrated at you."

"I am too. I wasn't in a good place after that long drive, not eating anything but chips."

"Let's promise that from now on, we have a good meal before we hit the road."

"Promise," Kait says as she ladles another bowl of stew for each of us. Although our moods have improved, we're both exhausted from the eight hours we spent on the road and head to bed.

"It's really warm in the bedroom," Kait says, throwing the covers off herself.

"I have the windows up front open and the fan on, but with the slides closed, we can't open the windows next to the bed."

"What about the emergency escape window? Can we open that?"

"I think so; let me check."

I can open the window and swing it upwards, but there's no way to hold it open. After thinking for a moment, I get out of bed and rummage through the trash. Crawling back onto the bed, I take my piece of trash and use it to prop the window open.

"There you go!" I say triumphantly.

"Did you really just use an empty beer can to prop the window open?" Kait asks, giving me a sideways look.

"Yep, and the breeze feels great."

TIP FROM THE ROAD: City ordinances are always changing so be sure to call ahead before arriving at a destination like a casino or Walmart to make sure they still allow overnight parking. The AllStays Camp and RV app is an essential tool and you can typically get recent notes from other RVers on their experiences. Check out our full review of the AllStays app here: https://weretherussos.com/allstays-camp-and-rv-app/

4. TOQUERVILLE FALLS

Thursday, September 17th, 2015

You may not believe it, but I had an amazing night's sleep. Shortly after we closed our eyes, a semi-trailer truck pulled in two spots over from us. The driver left the engine idling all night long, and that low rumble put me right into a deep sleep.

After a bowl of leftover pork stew for breakfast, I dropped a few more dollars in the slot machines and grabbed a coffee for the road. While I was inside, Kait found a Walmart along our route that allows overnight parking. After a quick call to the store in Hurricane, Utah, the manager confirmed that we could stay a night or two in their parking lot.

Morning rush hour in Vegas is just starting, but we don't hit much traffic. Kait's never driven past Vegas on Interstate 15, and this will be her first time in Utah. I've been out this way a couple times, the last being on my motorcycle. I was taking a road trip to see my friend, Jeremy, in Fort Collins and thought it would be a good idea to ride through the Nevada desert mid-summer with my leathers on. I don't think I was able to drink water fast enough to replace what I was losing while flying down the highway. Driving through the desolate desert now, I miss that adventure but realize it's much more comfortable with AC, a fridge full of snacks and a cup of hot coffee.

Just after noon, we pull into the Walmart in Hurricane (pronounced hur-A-kin). The manager told Kait we could park anywhere in the back of the parking lot and gave us permission to put our jacks down and slides out as long as we weren't blocking anything. We find a spot that's isolated between two grass medians, disconnect the Jeep and back the motorhome into the spot.

Before we hit the road, we read that there are businesses like Walmart that allow RVers to park overnight. We also read that some people were taking advantage of this courtesy and rather than spending a night, they would spend a week or more. Many of these people would also put out their lawn chairs, have BBQs and even dump their waste tanks onto the grass. Because of this, some Walmarts have now made it a policy not to allow overnight parking, and we read stories of people being kicked out of their lots by the police. By calling ahead, we're able to make sure we have permission and can sleep without worrying about getting a knock in the middle of the night.

Once we're settled, Kait heads inside to buy a few things, and I leash the boys for a walk. They drag me down the stairs and over to the bushes. Every time we get somewhere new, they sniff every inch while trying to pee on just about anything they can. We've only made it fifty feet before Kait walks back with her haul.

"What'd you get?" I ask as she walks over.

"I got some snacks for us and a couple treats for the boys since they've been so good. How far did you guys go?"

"This is it! They've sniffed every inch from here to the door."

"Well, it's a new place and they want to explore a bit."

"I know. Do you want to head out and do some exploring?"

"I'd love to, but do you think we're okay to leave the motorhome here?" Kait asks with a look of concern. "All of our stuff is in here, and what if someone breaks in or steals the motorhome?"

"I think we should be fine. There are enough people around that I doubt anyone will try breaking in. Let's just close all of the windows."

If someone did break in, we have a full-timer's insurance policy on the motorhome. It's similar to a homeowners policy and covers not only damage or loss to the motorhome but also our stuff inside. We can set the amount they cover for personal items and I set the limit pretty high. When I bought the policy, I was actually surprised that it was less expensive than what we were paying for our Jeep, even with the full-timers addition.

Getting the boys in the Jeep, we head out to scout the area. We're not far from Zion National Park so we drive there but stop short of the main entrance. They don't allow dogs on any trails, and Duke doesn't like being left in the Jeep, so we decide to skip it and just explore the area. The landscape is diverse with varying shades of red cliffs, sedimentary rocks and scrub brush. As we continue to explore, we find a few RV parks and a general store where Kait grabs a scoop of ice cream.

Around seven p.m. we head back to Walmart. As we approach the store, Kait begins to look a bit nervous. "What's wrong?" I ask.

"I don't see the motorhome."

"Honey, we parked on the other side of the lot. See?" I ask pointing to it as we come around the corner. "It's still there."

Kait breaths a sigh of relief once she confirms what I'm pointing to.

The next morning we're up early and pack the boys in the Jeep. When I went inside Walmart yesterday, the cashier suggested we check out Toquerville Falls. It's an hour drive to the falls and I'm excited. This is the first time we will have taken the Jeep on a 4x4 trail and I can't wait. I've wanted a Jeep ever since I saw them in <u>Jurassic Park</u> and have always dreamed of taking mine off-road.

As I am making my morning coffee, I look over and see Kait looking at her phone with a very concerned look. When I ask her what's wrong, she tells me that she was checking her bank account and panicked for a few moments because she didn't see her pay check deposited before she remembered that she's not getting them anymore. I hadn't even thought about that but now that she mentions it, this suddenly feels much more real.

Kait seems lost in thought, so I finish making my coffee and get the boys leashed up for our day out. Duke and Leo seem to sense my excitement and drag me to the Jeep. "Okay, okay, relax you two. Leo, you in first. Duke, wait your turn."

"The pull off is coming up," Kait says as we drive through the town of Toquerville on SR-17. The route takes us through residential streets until we reach a fence with a sign that reads "Extremely rough road 4WD recommended." Just past the sign, the asphalt fades into a dirt track and I put the

Jeep in four-wheel drive. I don't need to, but any excuse at this point will do.

The trail seems more like an unmaintained fire road, and after a few minutes we reach the first obstacle. There is a large mud pit with steep walls on either side and a rocky path on the opposite side.

As I begin accelerating towards the pit, Kait yells, "What are you doing?"

I don't respond. I just continue accelerating until we hit the mud pit. The windshield is immediately covered in mud, and I can't see anything. "Shit," I say holding the wheel tight as the Jeep threatens to veer off-course. We're through the pit in a few seconds, announced by the Jeep lurching over a few of the larger rocks.

"That was awesome!" I yell, giddy with laughter. Looking over I see Kait's white face. She's holding onto the grab bar in front of her and doesn't seem to want to let go.

"I just wanted to get the Jeep a bit muddy," I say.

"I can see that," Kait says, taking her hands off the grab bar. "Just warn me next time you do something like that."

"Okay," I respond with a devilish grin.

The windshield wipers are able to clear enough of the mud away so I can see again. Continuing along the trail, we run into a few more obstacles that require the four-wheel drive, but overall the road is in good shape. There are numerous turn-offs that lead to amazing views of the mountains and spots where people appear to have camped.

The boys don't seem to mind the rough road, and Duke has had his head out the window the entire drive. Leo is sitting in the back of the Jeep enjoying the ride and giving

Duke his space. We adopted Leo about two years after we got Duke. When they first met, Leo submitted to Duke right away and they got along great. Sure, there would be some growling here and there, but Duke never acted aggressively towards Leo. However, as Duke has gotten older, he's become a bit of a grumpy old man and doesn't like to share his space. Leo's realized this and has calmed down a lot around Duke. The two of them used to play quite bit, but now Duke just likes to lie down and sleep.

As we meander along the rough dirt road, I can see our bicycles in the rearview mirror swinging back and forth on the carrier we have attached to the Jeep's tow hitch. We haven't used them yet and they've been more of a pain in the butt than anything else. In order for me to access the back of the Jeep, I have to unlock the bikes and remove them from the carrier. While it's not difficult, it does take time and is making me rethink our decision to bring them.

"There are the falls," Kait says pointing past the dry creek bed we're driving on. A tame, meandering creek drops water over a rock cliff that people are walking across to a trail that continues to views of Zion.

"It's a good thing we have four-wheel drive here; otherwise we'd get stuck. This sand is pretty soft. I'm going to park over there on top of that rock so we don't have any problems getting out of here."

We spend a couple hours walking around the falls and relaxing. Duke is enjoying going back and forth through the water. Leo surprises both Kait and me by following Duke. In the past, anytime we've tried to take him to the water, he'd walk up, sniff it then run the other way. He is still very cautious about the water, but I think the fact that he sees Duke doing it is helping him get across.

"Ready to head home?" Kait asks as I come out of the creek with Duke.

"Sure, let's get the boys dried off and we can head back."

Kneeling down, I look under the Jeep and see mud caked into just about every crevice. "I saw a coin operated car wash in town. Let's stop there on the way back and I'll spray the Jeep down."

"Do we have to?" Kait asks. "The Jeep looks pretty badass like this. I feel like this is the way Jeep's are supposed to look."

"I love you so much right now."

"I'm serious!"

I explain to Kait that all of the mud caked to the underside of the Jeep can cause issues. Better to get it washed off now than deal with problems later. But I promise her that we can keep getting the Jeep muddy during our travels.

The drive back to SR-17 is uneventful, and I take it slowly crossing back through the mud pit. My little stunt earlier is going to cost me a handful of quarters and some time at the car wash to fix. Not that I really mind and I would certainly do it again.

After a late lunch, we decide to spend the rest of the day sitting outside at a coffee shop working. The boys seem worn out from our adventure and are happy to relax at our feet. While Kait works on our website, I'm busy putting together a post about our time at Toquerville Falls. This doesn't feel like work since I'm enjoying what we're doing and sharing our adventures with people.

"Excuse me," a man says as he walks over to our table and looks at Duke. "Is that a Belgium Malinois?"

"Yes, he is," I reply. Duke, as usual, is at my side and watching the man closely.

The man introduces himself, extending one hand to me and putting the other under Duke's chin for him to smell. We begin to chat about dogs and the man tells us he used to be a dog handler in the military and that's how he recognized Duke's breed.

"Do you two live around here?" The man asks.

"Huh, good question," Kait says and looks perplexed. "I guess you could say we live here now. We quit our jobs a few weeks ago, sold our house and now we travel full time in an RV. We came in yesterday and are going to be taking off tomorrow."

"Wow, that's pretty cool. Good for you two. Better to enjoy it now than when you're old like me. Anyway, I won't keep you two. I just had to come over and say hello to Duke. Enjoy your time here in Hurricane."

Once the man is gone, Kait looks at me and says, "I wasn't sure what to say when he asked where we lived."

"I think your answer was perfect. I mean, we are living here right now. In a few days, we'll be living somewhere else. It will probably be hard for some people to wrap their heads around that," I say.

The dogs begin to look a bit anxious, so we decide to head back to the motorhome, or I should I say "home." That's really what it is. I guess now we can say, "Home is where we park it."

BONUS CONTENT: For more info and directions to Toquerville Falls, check out the article I wrote for our website: https://weretherussos.com/toquerville-falls-utah/

5. MOAB

Saturday, September 19th, 2015

"I think we should head down to Moab today," Kait says as I get out of bed. "I found a great camping spot along the Colorado river, and I'd love to go to Arches National Park. I figure we can spend a few days in the area and then make our way into Colorado."

"I love Moab. I spent some time there with Jeremy when I met him and his brother to do some canyoneering. Arches is awesome, and I'd love to go back, but before we do any of that, I need to make a pot of coffee."

(A brief note: as many of you must be thinking, "Joe has a SERIOUS coffee problem." Well you'll be glad to know that I've cut back drastically. To the surprise of many, I now only have two cups a day, but I make sure to savor them. Okay, back to the story...)

By ten a.m. everything is packed, and Kait is in the driver's seat ready to go. We've only been on the road for a little over a week now, but I am really enjoying traveling in a motorhome. There is a large ledge in front of the passenger's seat that is low enough for us to prop our legs onto and stretch out. I especially love being a passenger and setting up a little snack station on the ledge while we're driving. Duke's favorite spot is right under my legs so he can look out the side window as we drive. Leo is happy pretty much anywhere, and this morning he's passed out on the couch as we pull away from the Walmart.

According to the GPS we have 327 miles until we arrive at our destination. On this section of I-70, the highway weaves through hills and there is a strong crosswind. The large, boxy structure of the motorhome acts like a sail, and it gets pushed around quite a bit by wind and passing semi-trucks. You need to have a firm grasp on that steering wheel, ready to correct as each gust cuts across the highway.

As we approach Moab on US-191, the GPS announces, "In one mile turn left onto Utah 128 West."

128 is a narrow, twisty, two-lane road with a large cliff wall on the north side and the Colorado River on the south side. Kait is staying under the speed limit, trying to be cautious going around the corners. Our twenty-nine-foot motorhome is fairly easy to maneuver, but there's little room for mistakes on a road like this. One stray car or truck that ventures over the double yellow could put us in the ditch that's running along the edge of the road.

The campground Kait found is only a mile and a half up the road. Once we reach it, there are large "Campground FULL" signs blocking the entrance. "What should I do?" Kait asks.

"I don't know, I guess keep going. I don't see a spot where we can pull in to turn around."

I'm not getting a cell signal so I can't look to see if there is a turnaround coming up. According to the GPS, the next cross road is about fifty miles further down this narrow, twisty road, and neither of us want to take a hundred-mile detour.

"What about that?" Kait asks, referring to a small pull-out on the left side of the road.

"It won't work. This road is too narrow for us to u-turn. We'd have to make a three-point turn and we can't reverse when we're towing the Jeep. Plus it'd be pretty dangerous if we were blocking the road, trying to make the turn."

Towing a car isn't like towing a trailer. Since the front wheels of the Jeep turn as we're driving, if we were to try and back up, the wheels would turn and the Jeep would make a tight turn in the wrong direction. The force of the motorhome going in one direction and the Jeep in another could damage the tow bar, the motorhome and the Jeep. We'll have to find a spot where we can pull over, disconnect the Jeep and turn around.

"There!" I yell, pointing to a narrow dirt pull-off on the right side of the road. The pull-out has just enough room for us to get off the road, and there is a small parking area on the opposite side of the road where we can turn around.

Kait pulls the motorhome over and asks, "Can you turn us around? I don't feel comfortable doing it, and you're better at backing up than I am."

"Of course. Why don't you get the Jeep disconnected and follow me in that. We can head back towards Moab and figure out another spot to camp for the night."

"Here, take one of the radios," Kait says as she hands me a walkie-talkie. During our research, many people suggested that you keep a set of walkie-talkies in the RV in case one person needs to help the other backup or maneuver into a tight spot. Since we aren't getting any cell signal, the walkie-talkies will allow us to talk to each other as we drive back towards town.

Once Kait has the Jeep disconnected, I wait for a break in the traffic and pull back onto the road.

"Are you sure you can make it? Over," Kait asks, over the radio.

"I think so, over," I reply to Kait, as I wait for a break in the oncoming traffic to make my turn. The parking area is narrow but there seems to be just enough space for me to pull in and turn around without blocking the road.

Pulling into the dirt lot, I realize it's smaller than I anticipated. Kait is still in the pull out across the road waiting in the Jeep. She has Leo with her, and Duke decided to stay with me. Duke seems confident I'll be able to pull this off. Leo, on the other hand, wasted no time following Kait out to the Jeep and is no doubt giving me a very unsupportive look from the backseat.

I pull as far into the parking area as I can, making sure the rear of the motorhome clears the road, then put the motorhome into reverse. There is a sheer drop-off into the river along the edge of the lot, so as I back up, I'm watching the rear camera and mirrors. In order to go far enough back, the overhang on the back of the motorhome is now hanging over the edge, and all I can see are rocks and rushing water in the camera. Switching to the mirrors, I watch the rear wheels to make sure they don't go off the edge.

"STOP!" Kait yells, over the radio. "You're about to go over the edge!"

"It's okay, I got it," I respond, and put the radio down. From her angle it probably looks like I was about to go off the edge, but I can see I still have a few more feet.

Since it's Saturday, the lot is packed with cars that are preventing me from making the turn and driving straight out, so I begin executing a three-point turn. Backing up once more, I'm able to get enough room to clear the cars and get back on 128.

"There's no way we could have done that with the Jeep attached," I say. "Where do you want to head?"

"There's supposed to be some BLM camping that we passed on the way into town off 191. Let's go check that out."

Passing the campground again, there is a large, forty plus foot motorhome with a long trailer that's slowed down to get into the campground. The driver is an older man and doesn't look too happy the campground is full. "Looks like the guy in that motorhome is going to have to turn around too," I say to Kait over the radio. "Poor guy. "He'll never be able to turn around in that spot we used, over."

Twenty minutes later we arrive at the turn off for BLM 378; a dirt road heading out into the desert. I pull the motorhome over to the edge of a large dirt area and get out with Duke.

"I don't want to take the motorhome down the road if we don't know what to expect," I say. "Let's take the Jeep, scout the area and, if we find anything, we can bring the motorhome in."

"Okay, hop in," Kait says.

Kait takes us down a few roads that look smooth enough for the motorhome, but all of the camping spots we find are already occupied. Dispersed camping is allowed on a lot of Forest Service and BLM land in "established" camping spots. This means that you're not just driving into some open field to camp, but rather using spots that have clearly been camped on previously. In this area campers are allowed to stay up to fourteen days before they have to move at least a few miles away before setting up camp again.

We find a lot of roads that are rutted out or too rocky to drive the motorhome on. We're worried that we may bottom out and break something or get stuck and have to pay an arm and a leg to get towed out.

"Look at that!" I exclaim, pointing at two large motorhomes parked on top of a rock outcropping. I have no idea how they even drove up there. The front wheels of each motorhome are on the rock, but the rear wheels have been lifted two or three feet off the ground in an attempt to try and level both rigs.

"Are those wood blocks they have under the hydraulic jacks?" Kait asks.

"Yep," I respond, wondering what might happen if the motorhome were to roll back and fall off the blocks.

Driving back to the motorhome, Kait and I decide to head back to a parking lot we saw that looks like it allows RV parking. When we pull up, I see a sign for 7 Mile Parking and another stating there is a nightly fee to park. There are already a few RVs parked there, including the large motorhome we passed earlier after our u-turn. I guess he managed to find a place to turn around.

After we level and set up, we take the boys for a walk to scope the area out and pay for our night of parking. The pay station is a steel pole with a slot you drop an envelope with your payment into. "I wonder if they ever check this?" Kait asks.

"Who knows? Let's write a check. That way if they don't cash it, we're not out any money. Plus we have a record of it if they do cash the check."

"I'm just happy that there is a place for us to park here."

"Me too. I was thinking about that on our drive here. We should try to avoid going to a new place on the weekend. I bet on Monday that campground will be empty."

"Oh, good point, I didn't even think about that. I forgot that we can show up any day of the week."

Walking past the large motorhome from earlier, the gentleman we saw driving is standing outside, so we decide to say hello.

"Where did you manage to turn that thing around," I shout.

"You mean back there on 128?" The man asks.

"Yeah, we had a hard time getting our rig turned around. I'm surprised you were able to."

"I wasn't about to drive another hour to the next road to turn around. I used to be a truck driver so I can pretty much turn around just about anywhere. I just jack-knifed the trailer and had no problem making the turn."

"Wow, I would have loved to have seen that. I'm Joe; this is my wife Kait."

"Howdy, nice to meet the two of you. I'm Eddie and my wife Sue is inside fixing up some dinner. How long have you two been on the road?"

"Just over a week now, but we're full-timers," Kait responds.

"A couple newbies!" Eddie laughs. "Don't worry, the two of you will get the hang of it. Sue and I hit the road about fifteen years ago. We used to have a bigger rig but we realized we didn't need something that size. So we bought this new and love it."

"What do you tow around in the trailer?" I ask.

"Mainly my 4x4 along with some extra things we store in there. Sue and I love to take some of the trails around here in Moab. Last year we took the trail that starts in this here lot and on the way back, we saw these two youngsters who looked half dead. I drove up and asked if they needed any water or wanted a ride out. The one almost started crying. They had hiked in, got lost and didn't bring enough water."

"Wow, good thing you found them!" Kait exclaims.

"Joe, Kait, this here is my wife, Sue," Eddie says pointing to the woman coming out of the motorhome.

We all chat for a while and learn that Eddie and Sue spend most of their time boondocking around the country and try to come back to this area every winter. They give us some pointers for places to camp in the area before we head back to the motorhome.

The next day we take the boys to Arches National Park. Unfortunately, dogs aren't allowed on any of the trails, so I hang out with them in the Jeep while Kait goes to see a few of the arches up close. I've been before, so I don't mind hanging back and walking the boys around the parking lot. Leo is especially annoyed I won't let him on any of the trails. Being a husky, he loves following trails, and each time we walk past one, he turns and wants to follow it. When I try to pull him along, he "speed bumps" by dropping to the ground and spreading his legs out, so I can't budge him. He can be a stubborn butt sometimes. On the complete opposite end of the spectrum, Duke's just happy to follow me around.

BONUS CONTENT: Here's an article we wrote about our time at Arches NP with the boys: https://weretherussos.com/toquerville-falls-utah/ At the end of the article, there's a link to more about the parking spot we stayed at. Also, check out our Travel Destinations page for all travel related articles: https://weretherussos.com/where-are-the-russos-travel-map

6. OVER THE ROCKIES

With Moab in our rearview mirror (well, if the motorhome had a rearview mirror), the drive took us back onto Interstate 70 and into Colorado. Our first stop was at the Visitor Center in Fruita to use their public RV dump and fill up with potable water.

In the eight days we've been on the road, our seventy-five-gallon water tank is only about half empty and our sixty-gallon gray tank is about half full. The forty-gallon black tank, where all the sewage ends up, is three-quarters full. We've done a great job conserving water by taking "Navy showers," (a quick shower where you get wet, turn the water off, soap up and then quickly rinse off) but it seems like the black tank is going to be our limiting factor when it comes to how long we can stay out before dumping.

Conservation is important to us because we don't plan on spending much time at campgrounds. The more we conserve, the longer we can camp without having to worry about finding a dump station. For people who like to spend the majority of their time at campgrounds with full hookups, conservation isn't something they need to be concerned with.

From the rest area, we continued to Eagle, Colorado, where we planned to spend the night. The fairgrounds allow free overnight parking, so we pulled alongside a few semi-trucks and settled in for the night to get some rest before attempting to go up and over the Rocky Mountains.

Tuesday, September 22nd, 2015

"Okay, ready to tackle the Eisenhower Tunnel today?" I ask Kait, as we're lying in bed listening to the neighboring semi-trucks idle.

According to the look on her face, she's not. She's worried that we're not going to make it over the pass as she's read some RVers avoid going this route because of the steep, long grade. Personally, I think we'll be fine. We might have to go slower than the rest of the traffic but I don't think we're going to have a problem. I took my motorcycle up this route a few years ago, and it's not as bad as people make it out to be.

"I know it's my turn to drive today, but could you please drive us?" Kait asks.

"Of course, I'd be happy to. I'm just going to need some coffee so I'm somewhat functional this morning. I honestly don't know how people function in the morning without it."

Kait laughs and as she gets out of bed says, "You know you have a problem, right?"

"Yep, and I love it."

Although I haven't let on to Kait, I'm a bit nervous myself. We have a 20,000-pound motorhome towing a 4,500-pound Jeep, and there is certainly some doubt in my mind that we'll make it over the mountain. Eisenhower Tunnel is one of the highest tunnels in the world at just over 11,000 feet. I've read the same comments online that Kait has, and I thought people were being silly for driving another route. I'm wondering now if that might have been a good idea.

We're on the road by 8:45 a.m. As we're making our way east on Interstate 70, I begin to think back to my previous life. Every Tuesday I had a morning staff meeting at about this exact time. We'd all gather at one of the many conference rooms in the building, discuss current project statuses, and everyone looked like they wished they were somewhere else. I used to look out the window and daydream about doing just about anything else except sitting there listening to people drone on about nothing. Now I'm living that dream. It feels very surreal because I haven't yet fully decompressed from that former life.

I'm also wondering what's in store for us once this adventure is over. We only planned to do this for one year. As much as I would like to keep going, the money we saved is going to run out. We might be able to cut back on certain expenses but at some point we're going to run out of money and have to go back to work.

"This drive is absolutely beautiful," Kait says, snapping me out of my daze. As usual, Duke has positioned himself right between Kait's legs and is admiring the view with her. Leo is passed out on the dog bed we have between our seats and could care less about what's going on. He's not a morning dog and doesn't like to be up before noon.

"Well, here we go," I say to Kait, as the interstate starts to rise at a much steeper grade. Until now I've been able to hold our speed coming up the hill, but the speedometer is quickly dropping despite the fact that I have the accelerator pinned to the floor. Each time the transmission downshifts, the engine takes on a whole new growl. Looking down, I see 4,500 RPM on the tachometer and reach over to put our hazard lights on.

"Is the engine going to make it?" Kait asks, with a very nervous look.

"I hope so. I don't know how long we can sustain this, but I do know one thing—our MPG is going to be horrible!" I yell over the roar of the Ford V10 gas engine. It's so loud that I can't hear Kait's response, and all of my attention is focused on the large dump truck ahead of us. The truck's blinkers are flashing, and the driver is only going about fifteen miles per hour. We're holding around thirty-five, and I am looking for an opportunity to move over and pass the truck before I have to slow down. I'm concerned that if I take my foot off the gas, we'll never get any speed back and be stuck behind the truck.

Two cars fly past and I take the opportunity to move over and pass the dump truck. Although it seems like it takes forever to get past the truck, we make it without losing any more speed. "One benefit of going this slow is we get to admire the gorgeous scenery!" Kait yells, once we're back in the right lane.

"Ha! Very true. We're not in a race, so I don't mind taking our time up the mountain. I just didn't want to be stuck behind that truck."

Continuing along Interstate 70, we pass Beaver Creek and Vail. We'd like to explore a lot of these little ski towns but we don't think we'd be able to find a place to park the motorhome. Instead, we put it on a running list Kait has started of places we want to come back to and explore.

Coming toward the Vail Summit Pass rest area, we decide to pull off, stretch our legs and give the engine a break. The lot is packed with cars, but we're able to snag an RV spot near the restrooms.

"I can't open the door," Kait says, as I am trying to get the boys leashed up for their walk.

"What do you mean? Did you unlock the deadbolt?"

"Yep, and I still can't get the door open."

"That's not good; let me try." I hand the boys' leashes over to Kait and try the handle on the door. I can turn it, but the door isn't opening. Holding the handle down, I slam into it with my shoulder, and the door pops open. "There you go. Why don't you head to the bathroom, and I'll walk the boys. We can switch when you get back."

"Okay, see you in a couple minutes."

As Kait walks towards the bathrooms, I turn to close the door and find that it won't shut. I can't examine it because the boys are trying to drag me to a patch of grass across the lot. I leave the door and walk over with them, keeping an eye on the motorhome to make sure no one tries to go inside.

"What's wrong?" Kait asks, walking towards us.

"The door won't close."

"What? How is that possible?"

"I don't know. Let me run over to the bathroom; then I'll take a look."

When I get back, Kait and the boys are standing outside the motorhome. "What are we going to do if we can't get the door closed?" Kait asks with a worried look.

"Let's not worry about that now. Let me take a look at it and see what's going on."

Looking closer I notice that the edge of the door is hitting the end of the striker bolt, preventing the bolt from engaging with the door latch. Somehow the motorhome twisted or shifted just enough so the bolt is a couple millimeters off. No matter how hard I try to force the door, there's no way I can get it closed.

"Let's give Newmar a call and see what they say," I suggest. "This is definitely a warranty issue, but I don't know what we're supposed to do all the way up here. There's no way we can drive the motorhome if we can't close the door."

A few minutes later, the woman in customer service transfers me to the person who handles warranty issues with the Bay Star models.

"Hi, Joe, this is Brad. How can I help you today?"

"Hey, Brad, my wife and I have a bit of a problem." I explain the issue to Brad and he seems genuinely concerned. As I take a closer look at the bolt while talking to him, I notice something.

"Brad, I just noticed that I can unscrew the bolt. I have the tools to do it. Do you think it would be safe to remove the bolt and use the deadbolt to keep the door closed until we can get it fixed?"

"Hold on, Joe, I want to check with one of the technicians and see what they say. It might take a few minutes, so let me call you back once I have an answer."

Within a few minutes, Brad is back on the phone and tells me that my suggested band-aid would work until we got to a Newmar service center. He says there is a dealer we can drive to just outside of Fort Collins or he can send a mobile technician to our location, but that would take a few hours.

"I'm confident I can get the bolt out," I tell Brad. "We'd prefer to keep driving and stop at the dealer. When do you think they can get us in?"

"I gave them a call before I called you back. They're expecting you whenever you can make it in. They close at five, so you should have more than enough time to make it there today. If you have any other problems, don't hesitate to call me back."

I thank Brad and fill Kait in on the situation.

"Wow, their customer service is really good," Kait says. "So you think you can get the bolt out?"

"Should be easy," I say.

Grabbing my tools, I pull out the correct size socket and ratchet. I'm thankful I decided to bring them all. I wondered if having this many tools was overkill, but they're certainly worth having at a time like this.

Once I get the bolt out, I realize that I might be able to fix this myself. Going back into the bay where I keep all of my tools, I grab a few bags of random nuts, bolts and washers. Whenever I had a spare that I thought I might need at some point, I put it in one of these bags. I threw a lot of these bags in the trash when we were clearing out the garage, but a few found their way into my toolbox. Looking through the first one, I find what I need. Two steel washers that fit perfectly over the door bolt I'm holding in my hand.

The bolt is only off by a couple millimeters, so I slide both washers over the threads and screw the bolt back into the door frame. Kait is inside watching me, holding onto the boys so they don't try running out the door. She's been very concerned about the door but is now looking at me with fascination.

Tightening the bolt, I hold my breath and close the door. To my delight the door closes with a solid "thunk" and opens right back up without any issue.

"Door's fixed," I say with a triumphant smile on my face.

"What did you do?"

"Well, remember all of those bags of nuts and bolts you told me to throw out? I kept a few and had the right size washers in there to shim the bolt. It works perfectly now," I say, opening and closing the door.

"I'm impressed, but I still think we should go to the dealer and have them take a look at it."

"I agree. I don't want this happening again."

A short while after leaving the rest area, we finally come to the top and see the Eisenhower tunnel. Although the engine has been screaming the whole way up, the temperature gauge reads normal, and I have a feeling the motorhome could have done this all day.

Before we left this morning, Kait asked if she should detach the Jeep and drive separately. Part of me thought it was a good idea, but the other part wanted to see if the motorhome could actually make it. Now that we're up, I feel proud of our motorhome and triumphant that we're now driving through the tunnel. My positive feelings soon turn back to anxiety when I notice the steep grade sign for the trip down the other side of the mountain.

As we make our way down the mountain, the grade begins to get steeper. Every time I let off the brakes, the motorhome quickly picks up speed. I've read that if the brakes get too hot, they begin to fade, preventing the motorhome from stopping. To combat this, I downshift the motorhome into a lower gear and use the engine to help manage our speed. The RPMs shoot up but the motorhome is now holding at a steady speed.

About halfway down the mountain, traffic starts backing up. We didn't expect that we'd hit traffic on a Tuesday, but maybe everyone took a long vacation and are now driving home. Either way, I really have to go to the bathroom, and there's no place we can pull over.

"I have to pee bad. Take over and drive while I go. I can't wait."

"Um, okay. How are we going to do this?"

"As soon as traffic comes to a stop, I'll run back and you can take over."

"Alright, I'm ready," Kait says.

With Kait in the driver's seat, I can use the bathroom, except traffic is constantly slowing and accelerating making things...difficult. The experience reminds me of being in an airplane and trying to go while bouncing around in some serious turbulence.

"Oh, I feel so much better. Want to switch back?"

"Sure, but let's wait until traffic comes to a stop again."

At 1 p.m. we arrive at the Newmar dealer. The receptionist tells me that they got the call from Brad and can take a look at the door for us. We walk out to the motorhome so she can see the problem and write up a work order.

"Thank you for taking us. This has been really stressful," I tell her. "I didn't think we'd have problems with a new motorhome."

"Oh no problem, we're happy to help. What all is wrong besides the door?"

"Uh, nothing I can think of at the moment. The screen door is also out of alignment a bit but everything else is fine."

After a short laugh, the receptionist looks at me and says, "Honey, listen. I have customers come in here with pages of issues they need fixed on new motorhomes. If the door and screen are your only problems, you're doing real good."

Looking at the door, I explain the fix I made to the latch and show her that the screen door won't stay closed anymore. She examines it for a second, closes the door, opens it and laughs again.

"I'm happy to have one of my techs look at this, but you did the same thing they would have to fix it. I don't think there is anything else they need to do. As for the screen, all you need to do is loosen this screw and adjust the latch for it to close. All you need is a Phillips."

I must have a skeptical look on my face because she laughs again and says, "I used to work in service, and it's a pretty common problem."

"Ah, ok, I have a few screwdrivers. I can take care of the screen myself. Sorry to waste your time, I just didn't know if there was something else the techs could do with the door."

"No problem. If it gives you any more issues, bring it back in and we'll take a look, but you're good to go."

Going back into the motorhome, Kait looks visibly relieved. "Thank you for fixing the door," she says. "I was worried that we were going to have to leave the motorhome here so they could fix it."

"You're welcome. Now we have to figure out where to spend the night. Jeremy and Christine live in an apartment, so we can't park outside their place."

On our drive here, Kait was looking online and saw that Fort Collins doesn't allow overnight parking in public lots like Walmart. She did however find some dispersed camping spots around the area and a few campgrounds. We decided to park the motorhome at Walmart and take the Jeep around to scout the area.

We haven't been on the road long but trying to figure out where we're going to sleep each night is starting to stress me out. It doesn't seem to bother Kait, but I start getting stressed when we head to a new place. Will we find a place we can park overnight? Will we have to drive around for hours to find something? Will we get kicked out by the police? All things I worry about. Since we haven't stayed anywhere more than a few nights, it would be nice if we could find a place to relax for a bit longer and not have to worry about finding that next place.

When we were planning this adventure, we didn't budget much for campgrounds because we'd read about various places we could camp for free. We also didn't have a schedule so we didn't have to worry about trying to book campgrounds in advance. Our plan was to do as much free camping as possible to help stretch our funds and move when we wanted. Now, I'm starting to wonder if we should just spend money on a campground for a few nights rather than stress over where we're going to overnight next.

BONUS CONTENT: Here's more about our trip over the Rockies along with some photos of the drive and me repairing the door: https://weretherussos.com/70-east-drive-in-a-rv/

7. LOSING A FRIEND

Wednesday, September 23rd, 2015

Colorado is beautiful, and one of the places I was most looking forward to visiting was Fort Collins. Little did I know that after last night, this would be the place I had to leave my friend behind. What did I think, that hitting the road and leaving my old life behind meant rainbows and butterflies everyday? Life still happens and we got a reminder of how quickly things can go south and tough decisions need to be made.

"Why don't we go grab a beer?" Kait asks, putting her arm around me.

"Great idea, I could really use one right about now. Come on, Leo, back in the Jeep."

Craft beer has become huge in the United States over the last few years, and Fort Collins is one of the hotspots. The last time I was in Fort Collins, Jeremy and I went brewery hopping and one of my favorites was New Belgium. Even in the afternoon on a weekday, it tends to be quite busy, just the distraction Kait and I need right now.

"Can we bring our dog into the brewery?" Kait asks, after we see a few pups running around the bar.

"Of course, they're more than welcome," the bartender replies.

Kait and I grab a seat at the bar while Leo basks in the attention. White Huskies are rare, and with his ice blue eyes, people are always drawn to Leo. He loves the attention, and while he's being loved on by strangers, Kait and I order a flight of tasters.

"To Duke," I say, holding up my first taster.

"Our boy," Kait responds, with a tear in her eye.

Taking a long sip, I look down at the bar and say, "I know we've only been on the road for ten days, but today is going to be one of the toughest times we'll have."

We knew that Duke didn't have much time left and this day would come, but I always felt like he would live forever. He had a rough life before we found him, but since then he's had an amazing eight years with us. Even though it's only been ten days, he got to see so much more than most dogs do and I could tell he loved it.

"Now we just have to make sure and spoil Leo as much as we can," Kait says, putting her arm around me.

With tears rolling down my cheeks, I start laughing. Since we left the vet's office, Leo seems to have perked up. I think he knew Duke hadn't been doing well and has been very restrained around him. Now that he's gone, that light in Leo seems to be back.

Turning around in my seat, I look outside to remind myself how beautiful this place is and I'm content to know my friend will rest here. When we made the appointment, we opted for a communal cremation for Duke. They told us his ashes would be disposed of locally, and we were happy to know we'd be leaving him in such a beautiful place.

Turning back around, I nod toward the flight and ask, "Which one's your favorite?"

"I like them all, but the Sunshine Wheat is my favorite. You?"

"The Voodoo Ranger IPA," I say staring at the row of now half full glasses.

"What's wrong?" Kait asks.

"I don't know. I've just been sitting here thinking about things. With everything we've been through today I realized that I miss being someplace familiar. It's hard to have to put your dog down, but it's even more difficult when you're in an unfamiliar area. I called three or four places this morning before we found a vet that would take us. I'm enjoying all the new things, but at the same time I miss that familiarity of home. Having our spots, like our favorite Chinese takeout spot that was down the street."

"Do you want to stop and move back to Los Angeles?" Kait asks with a worried look.

"No, I think I just need some time to adjust and get used to this. I also feel very lonely. I love being able to spend all this time with you, but I miss our friends and family. It's strange to say, but I miss going into work and being around everyone. I miss that social interaction. I didn't realize it until we came in here. Just sitting here, being around people has been very therapeutic for me. Maybe we should try to get out a bit more and mingle with the locals."

"I think that's a great idea. Plus, we're meeting Jeremy, Christine and Will tonight, so you can get your friend fix. Anything else bothering you?"

"Well, since you asked, there is one more thing. Trying to find a place to park where we can spend the night is starting to stress me out. Every time we go somewhere, we have to look places up, call ahead and try to find somewhere that will let us park. Even then we can only do it for a night or two before we have to leave and find another spot. I know we're trying to save money by not staying at campgrounds, but like tonight, we have no idea where we're going to stay."

"That's tough for me too," Kait says. "When I called Walmart yesterday, they told me that there is a city ordinance that prevents overnight parking. However, I found a place to stay," Kait says, pulling up the map on her phone. "The Cracker Barrel allows overnight parking for customers, and they have RV parking in the back.

"Wait, you said there is a city ordinance that prohibits overnight parking."

"Yes, but the woman I spoke to said they aren't affected by that because they own the lot. Same reason why we were able to spend last night at the Budweiser plant."

"Huh, interesting," I say. "Well, I love Cracker Barrel and their hash brown casserole."

"I've never been. What else is good there?"

"Really? Everything on their menu is good, but the casserole is my favorite. I know where we're going for breakfast tomorrow."

"Look at that," Kait says, nudging me in the ribs. I turn to follow her gaze and see a group of women at the bar. While this normally wouldn't be anything out of the ordinary, each one has a baby with them. I see a couple in strollers but most have their baby in one of those slings and are ordering beers. We overhear one of the women asking her friend if she brought the alcohol test strips for her breast milk.

"That's something you don't see most places," I chuckle and take the last sip of our flight.

As we get ready to leave, I'm feeling much better. It's going to take a while, but I'm at peace now and can move forward. We decide to head back to the Budweiser brewery and move the motorhome to Cracker Barrel. They were very generous letting us park there overnight after the tour, but I don't want to push our luck.

Pulling up to Cracker Barrel, I see a sign indicating RV parking and follow the arrow to the back of the restaurant. There are multiple large, pull-through parking spots for RVs or tour buses. I pick one alongside a grass median so we can safely put our bedroom slide out and park.

"Let's go in and introduce ourselves to the manager," Kait suggests.

"Okay," I say and turn in my seat to face Leo. "You going to be alright in here by yourself?" I ask him.

Leo snorts, does a little spin and jumps onto the couch. "I guess that's a yes," Kait says with a huge smile.

Walking through the door to Cracker Barrel, Kait is overwhelmed by the large gift shop that greets us. They have just about every candy, old-fashioned sodas, toys and knick-knacks you can think of. We spend a few minutes walking around in awe of everything they have.

"Oh, apple butter, I love this stuff," I tell Kait, holding up the jar to show her. Having gone to school in Indiana, I'm familiar with all the Midwest goodies and have missed warm banana bread with fresh apple butter and a pinch of cinnamon.

"Can we speak to the manager?" Kait asks the hostess who looks slightly concerned she's done something wrong.

"Sure, one moment."

A few minutes later, the manager comes over to introduce himself. He also looks a bit concerned and apprehensive about why we've asked to see a manager.

Kait explains that she spoke to someone over the phone about staying the night with our RV. She tells the manager we just wanted to say hello and will be coming by for breakfast in the morning.

The manager looks relieved and thanks us for coming in. He says he'll be here in the morning and looks forward to seeing us. He also assures us the lot is safe, and there are police who patrol regularly.

Walking back out to the motorhome, I look over at Kait and say, "I think we're going to need to be more specific when we ask for a manager."

"Why? He seemed happy that we introduced ourselves."

"He looked relieved. I think he was worried we were going to complain about something. Typically, when someone asks to see the manager, it's because they want to complain about something."

"Oh, good point. I didn't even think about that, but now that you mention it, you're right. He did look a bit nervous."

"I don't know about you, but now that we have the motorhome settled, I wouldn't mind just kicking back and relaxing for a bit before we meet everyone for dinner."

"I'm really looking forward to seeing everyone and meeting Will. Do you remember how old he is?"

"I think he's around two. Jeremy said we could bring Leo. Will loves dogs."

That evening we drive over to Christine and Jeremy's apartment to meet everyone.

TALES FROM THE OPEN ROAD

"CHOOO CHOOO!" Will yells as we walk in their apartment.

"Sorry," Christine says, grabbing Will. "He just learned about trains and can't stop making his whistle noise. We're trying to get him to stop."

"Oh, we don't mind," Kait says, smiling.

"You will after he does it about a hundred times."

"So where do you want to go?" I ask.

"I was thinking we can go downtown. There are a few places that have outdoor patios so you can bring Leo."

Once we get downtown, Christine and Jeremy take us on a short walking tour of the area. As we stroll past shops and restaurants, Jeremy and I chat about life and it feels like old times. It makes me realize how lonely I've felt on the road and how much I needed this time with an old friend. They really helped get our minds off the day and truly relax for an evening. It's just what we needed.

The next morning, we head into Cracker Barrel for breakfast. Kait gets sausage patties and the hashbrown casserole I couldn't shut up about. I get Grandpa's Country Fried breakfast with casserole, of course. Over a couple rounds of the triangle peg game they have at every table, Kait asks me what is in my breakfast and I tell her chicken fried steak. "How can a steak be chicken fried?" She asks. After a bit of laughter, I explain to her that it's a thin slab of steak that's breaded, fried and covered in gravy.

After breakfast, Kait says, "We may have to be careful how often we stay at Cracker Barrels. That was great but I'll be 100 pounds overweight if we keep this up."

"I know what you mean. I probably just gained five pounds. What do you want to do today?"

"Let's head to the coffee shop. I have a lot of work I want to get done on our website and a couple articles to write," Kait says.

"Let's find one with a nice patio so we can sit outside with Leo."

When we arrive at the coffee shop, the place is packed, but Kait manages to find a table outside next to an outlet. I head inside to order a coffee for myself and an ice water for Kait. The nice thing about working from some coffee shops is I get free (or discounted) coffee refills.

Before she starts working, Kait suggests we sell the bicycles, and I agree to post them on Craigslist. We still haven't used them, and it seems pointless to drag them around the country, so I walk over to the Jeep, snap a few pictures and list the two bikes along with the carrier as a package deal.

Kait is lost in her work for the next few hours. She occasionally asks me to do something, but for the most part, I've been surfing the web. I'm surprised how much time she's been putting into the website. We've talked about the fact that I'm not ready to dive back into work a few times. However, I can see her starting to become stressed about my lack of participation. This has become Kait's new full-time job. Granted, there are people out there who make quite a bit of money off of their websites, but I'd be amazed if we ever get enough traffic on the site to even cover the $600 per month payment we have on the motorhome.

I've also caught Kait looking at job openings for remote positions. When I asked about it, her response was that she was considering finding a job so we could afford to keep doing this. While I appreciate the idea, it also makes me a bit upset. We did this to get away from work and spend a year together seeing the country. If Kait were to start working, she'd be busy all day while I relaxed or went out. I can't see that lasting long before she began to resent me for not working, and that's the last thing I would want.

"You ready to go?" Kait asks without looking up at me.

"Sure, if you are," I reply gingerly.

I can tell she's upset because of my lack of participation on the website. To be honest, it's really not something I want to do. I tried my own blog years ago about motorcycles, but I didn't enjoy it, and I have no interest in writing articles now for our website. That said, I have contemplated making YouTube videos. It seems like much more fun, and as I watch different vlogs I follow, I keep thinking, "we can do that." What's been stopping me from trying is on our last day of work, we filmed a vlog. It was supposed to be our first in a series about our adventures, but I had nothing to say and did not like having the camera in my face. When it was over, I told Kait I never wanted to do that again, but the more I think about it, the more I want to try again. Plus, I think it would be fun editing the videos and telling our story to the world.

I mentioned this idea to Kait, but her concern is that there's so much more to it than making a video. We can't just upload them and hope people watch. We'd need to figure out how to get YouTube to promote our videos through optimizing titles, descriptions and keywords for the search engines. We'd also need to find a niche and stick with it. That can be product reviews, places we go in the RV, whatever, but we would need to be consistent so people know what to expect.

At the end of the discussion, after rubbing her temples for a few moments, Kait said, "Why don't you look into it and put a plan together? If you're up for doing some work, I could use help with writing articles for the website."

When we get back to Cracker Barrel, we have a neighbor. Someone's pulled up with a fifth wheel trailer, and it looks like they are spending the night as well. Typically, businesses ask that you only stay a single night, but when we went into breakfast this morning, the manager came by to see how things were. When Kait thanked him for allowing us to stay, he graciously offered to let us to stay a second night. He said they're not very busy this time of year and we were welcome to stay.

"Guess what?" I say to Kait with mild bewilderment. "Someone already sent me a note about the bikes and wants to meet tonight to buy them."

"Wow, that was quick. I guess Fort Collins is a good market to sell used bikes."

"I guess so. Why don't I call this guy and have him come get the bikes? Then we can have dinner."

"That'd be great. I'm happy someone else is going to get some use out of them. Since we'll have some extra cash, maybe we can get breakfast again tomorrow," Kait says with a grin. "I grabbed a map from the restaurant this morning that has all the different locations where they allow overnight parking. I have a feeling it's going to come in handy."

BONUS CONTENT: While we had a very emotional time in Fort Collins dealing with the loss of Duke we decided that despite this, we'd have a great time with Leo. That led us to do a bit of brewery hopping with our white fluff ball who thoroughly enjoyed himself. Here's an article about the different places we went: https://weretherussos.com/best-breweries-in-fort-collins/

ROAD TIP: Various businesses around the US allow overnight parking for customers. Here's an article we put together about parking at Cracker Barrels overnight: https://weretherussos.com/boondocking-at-cracker-barrel/

8. THE PULL OVER

Thursday, October 8th, 2015

It's been less than a month since we hit the road, and I'm beginning to wonder how much longer we can go. The first week was everything I imagined. We'd wake up late, enjoy relaxed mornings and then take the boys out for the day. Since then, I noticed we were getting progressively more annoyed and frustrated with each other for little things like hanging up a towel the wrong way.

It reminded me of when we moved into our house. Things were great at first and then we started biting each other's head off over nothing, until one day it boiled over. What we realized was that we needed to learn how to live with each other. We'd been living together for almost two years before we bought the house, but we'd both been on our best behavior and were overlooking a lot of things that bothered us. Once we acknowledged the problem and talked through what was bothering each of us, life went back to normal. We just needed to get on the same page.

The problem now is I can't figure out what's bothering Kait. When I ask what is wrong, she either ignores me or tells me everything is fine. In response, I've been getting frustrated and annoyed. I know we can't go on like this. Eventually, history will repeat itself and things will boil over again. I've been worried that when they do, it might spell the end of the trip if we can't figure out how to work through it.

While we were still in the planning stages, people speculated that we may hate this lifestyle and would ask what we would do if it didn't work for us. We always told them that if we hated it, we would call it quits, take a hit on the motorhome and go back to our old lives. However, now that we've been on the road, I don't know if that would be possible. The problem we're having is with each other, not the lifestyle. If we can't work out what's causing us to feel this way, I'm worried that it may cause us to split up and go our separate ways. Some people just can't be around each other 24/7.

Even with all of this, we've been having a great time on the road. After getting to Fort Collins, we went through the Rocky Mountain National Park where Leo almost ate a squirrel and we got to hear and see the elks bugling. It was an awe-inspiring experience but the temperature in Colorado has been dropping, so we headed south to Pueblo and visited an air museum there. I'm a huge fan of airplanes, especially warbirds, so I told Kait I would write an article for our website about the place. She seemed excited that I was back in the mood to work, and I thought this would be a good way to ease back into it.

Things were almost back to normal for a few days and then she began asking about the article. We made it to Pagosa Springs a few days ago, and after being asked multiple times, I got the article done and showed it to her. I thought Kait would have been happy, but instead she re-wrote it and told me not to bother with the next one. Frustrated, she looked at me over her laptop and said, "It's going to take me more time to fix this than it would take for me to just write it." When I asked what needed fixing she just brushed me off, so I confronted her. She explained I had numerous grammar mistakes, misspellings and the flow was all wrong. Most of all, she was frustrated that she had to keep nagging me to write the article. I listened to her critique closely, and she was completely right. I wrote the article more like a diary entry rather than a piece for a professional travel site.

In my mind, weretherussos.com was a casual blog where people can come and follow our adventures. We talk about what we do each day, how we're feeling and where we are. Kait, on the other hand, views the website as more of an online resource for people. Give people searching for the Pueblo Weisbrod Aircraft Museum, for example, all the information they need: price, types of exhibits and our thoughts about it. This difference in opinion of our website has become another thing that we seem to be butting heads over.

When we left Pagosa Springs this morning, we were in good spirits. We'd spent a few days at our first RV park and really enjoyed being able to take some time off from boondocking and relax in one area for almost a week. I can't tell you how nice it was going into the bathhouse and taking a long, hot shower compared to the quick Navy showers we've been taking in the motorhome. Even with full hook-ups, our six gallon hot water heater doesn't allow us to take a shower longer than a few minutes.

The town itself was cute, but the real draw was the hot springs. A few resorts offer spas you have to pay to use, but instead we found a couple public springs along the river. Nothing better than sitting in a hot spring, then jumping in the freezing river to cool off.

We left Pagosa Springs about thirty minutes ago, and, aside from asking me to post a photo of our drive on Instagram, Kait hasn't said a word to me.

"Do you want me to put some music on?" I ask.

"Whatever," she says, not taking her eyes off the road.

"Is everything okay?"

"I'm fine."

"It doesn't seem like it. You haven't talked to me since we left the campground, and you look like you're in a bad mood."

"I just don't feel like talking."

I know she's upset at me, but I have no idea what I said, did or didn't do to set her off. Regardless, I'm tired of the silent treatment, and when we stop in Cortez later, I'm going to sit down with Kait and have a serious discussion about what's been going on between us. Thinking about it is making me nervous, but it's time for us to sit, talk and try to work things out. In the meantime, I'm just going to sit here, listen to my music and try to relax.

Shortly after we get through Durango, Kait puts her turn signal on and begins slowing for an upcoming rest area. We haven't spoken since our last exchange, and I don't know if we're pulling over so she can go to the bathroom, leave me here or both.

After she parks the motorhome, she gets up and walks outside towards the restrooms. Leo is excited so I leash him up and we head outside so he can visit the bushes. Once Leo is done, I turn to see Kait walking back towards us.

Kait stops in front of me and says in a very matter-of-fact voice, "I'd like to sit down and talk."

"So would I," I respond, and start walking back toward the motorhome, but Kait stops me.

"Let's sit over there," she says, pointing to the picnic table furthest away from where everyone is parked. My heart starts racing. I don't know what's going to happen, but I do know that when we leave this place, things will have changed.

I sit across from her at the concrete table, crossing my hands in front of me. Leo crawls under the table to curl up in the shade. Kait has her hands in her lap with her eyes closed, head down. I can see the strain on her face, and it looks like she is trying to compose herself before saying anything. Since I have no idea where this conversation is going, I decide to let Kait take the lead.

After a minute, Kait opens her eyes, looks up at me and says, "I don't feel like we're on the same page."

"In what way?"

"You seem like you're on vacation. Just having fun, reading your books and surfing the web while I do all the work. I'm writing the articles for our site, posting on Facebook and Instagram, handling our content schedule and everything that needs to be done to run a website."

"Look, I needed some time off. I talked to you about that, but I've started helping."

"Yes, but I have to keep asking you for help. Just like today. Did you ever post on Instagram?"

"Not yet."

"That's what I mean," Kait says with tears in her eyes. "You don't take the initiative to do any of this without me asking you, and I'm tired of pestering you. This has really been stressing me out, and today I realized that you and I just aren't on the same page."

"Hold on. I know we talked about trying to make some money off of the website, but I didn't think the plan was to turn it into a full-time job. The entire point of this trip is for us to be able to step away from work for a year and take time off. Instead, when we hit the road, you went right back into work mode."

After a long pause, Kait says, "You're right. I automatically went back into work mode. I think it's because I've been working since I was sixteen, and I'm finding it hard to turn that part of myself off." Kait takes another long pause before continuing. "I want our website to be successful and make enough so that we can stay on the road and not go back to our old lives, but you don't seem to feel the same way."

As soon as Kait's done talking, I feel a sense of relief wash over me. I realize we're both stressed about the same thing. It's the thought of having to go back. Back to the lives we left behind. Even if it's in some other place, we'll still need to go back to working for someone else. I think I've been burying myself in books and the Internet so I didn't have to face the reality that in less than a year, I would be sending out résumés again. Rather than bury her head in the sand, Kait went to work to keep us from having to face that reality.

"I'm really sorry," I say. "I had no idea your intention was to build the website so we don't have to go back to an office."

"Thank you," Kait says with tears rolling down her cheeks. She covers her face in her hands and begins sobbing. "This has really been eating away at me. I wanted to be able to let you just enjoy yourself, but I can't do everything on my own. That's why I was looking for remote jobs. I figured if I could make enough to keep us going, you could just sit back and relax."

I take a moment and realize what an amazing person Kait is. She's been more worried about me and my happiness than her own.

"I'm really sorry," I say, sitting up. "I've been in vacation mode trying to decompress from all those years at work while you've been back at work trying to keep us on the road. I don't want you to get a job because the reason we did this was to get away from all of that and spend time with each other. I want this to work, and I'm willing to put in the time with you."

Kait wipes her face and looks up at me with a smile. Her eyes are still red, but she seems relieved and says, "Ever since we left, I've felt this amazing freedom. For the first time, I don't have to answer to anyone else, and I don't want to give that up. I think that if we really put in the time, we can turn the website into a business, but it's going to take both of us to do it."

I walk over to Kait and give her a huge hug. "Thank you," I say. "I needed this kick in the ass to get me going. I've been stressing a lot recently about what's going to happen in eleven months when we need to start looking for jobs again. I don't want to go back to working for someone else and, like I said, I'm willing to put in the time it takes."

"I'm so happy to hear you say that because this wasn't working for me," Kait says.

"It wasn't working for me either," I tell Kait and she looks a little surprised.

"What do you mean?"

"Well, we've both been getting angry at each other over stupid things and neither of us has been talking about it. Plus, anytime you get upset and I ask what's wrong you just say 'nothing.' We live in a small space and are around each other 24/7. When we have problems, we have to communicate with each other."

"I'm sorry," Kait responds. "I have a bad habit of just shutting down when something bothers me. When I asked you to post on Instagram earlier, you told me you were busy looking something up and you'd do it later. It was the straw that broke the camel's back because I'm always taking pictures when you're driving but whenever I drive, I have to nag you to do it. Plus, I knew you'd forget and I would have to remind you."

"I'll work on being more proactive with things like that."

I give Kait another big hug. She starts crying again and I squeeze her even tighter. I can feel all the tension and anger leaving her body as she begins to relax and that sense of relief washes over me again. When we first sat down and I saw that look on Kait's face, I figured there was a 50/50 chance that this was it. We both needed this talk and while we'll probably continue to butt heads, I have a feeling that things going forward will be much smoother.

When I let go of Kait, she takes a few steps back and I see the person who was so excited to start this amazing journey with me a few weeks ago. This is the love of my life and I'll do anything to keep the two of us on the road traveling and living the life we want.

"So do you really think the website can earn enough money to cover all of our expenses?" I ask Kait, sitting back down.

Kait thinks for a minute before responding. "I don't know. There are a few food bloggers out there that I follow who make their living from their sites. But, food blogs are pretty popular and I don't know how many people out there are interested in RV life. I think we can do it, it's just going to take a lot of work."

"Well, I'm ready for it," I say. "Ready to get back on the road and get to Cortez?"

"Yes, I just need another hug."

After our hug, I look at Kait and say, "Thank you again. I really needed that kick in the butt."

"You're welcome, honey and thank you for talking to me. I didn't know how you'd take it but I needed to get all of that off my chest."

"So did I. I now have a renewed sense of excitement for the rest of this trip."

"Me too, but stop calling it a trip. It's no longer a trip, it's our life."

BONUS CONTENT: We put together a guide of RV living tips to help others survive the transition to RV life: https://weretherussos.com/rv-living-tips/

9. GRAND CANYON

Sunday, October 11th, 2015

When we drove into the Desert View entrance of Grand Canyon National Park yesterday, there were signs posted that all of the campgrounds were full. After our experience in Moab, we'd vowed to not arrive at a campground on a weekend, but how quickly the mind forgets, and here we were again with no idea where we would spend the night. Kait suggested we drive to the campgrounds anyway and see if there were any last-minute cancellations.

Desert View campground was the first one we saw, so I parked the motorhome in the registration area, and Kait went to investigate. The ranger at the office explained none of the campgrounds had any availability because it was one of their busiest times of year. She did suggest that we try back each day because they have cancellations, and if we wanted to, we could drive through the campground to check it out. Neither of us had ever been to a national park campground, so we took the ranger up on her offer.

Driving through was a mistake. The campground is arranged by loops all connected to a main road. As we drove into the campground, we realized there wasn't enough room for us to turn around since we were still towing the Jeep. We figured we'd just drive through the last loop which would spit us back out onto the main road towards the exit for the campground.

As I began driving through the loop, I realized why there is a thirty-foot restriction at this campground. It's not because the sites are small; it's because of how tight the loop roads are. They are narrow, one-way roads with trees on either side that leave little, if any, room to maneuver. We thought we had a small motorhome until we tried driving through this campground.

Proceeding around the loop, I carefully navigated between the tree branches, trying not to tear a hole in the roof or rip off the AC unit. Kait was diligently watching for branches when a loud scrape along the side of the motorhome made us realize we weren't careful enough. A rogue branch had put a scratch along the side of our motorhome. It wasn't bad but bothered me quite a bit considering the motorhome is still new, and I was becoming frustrated over not having a place to spend the night.

After leaving the campground, we headed to the main visitors center to regroup. According to the map, there was RV parking there. However when we arrived, the RV parking was completely full. Most of the spots were taken by cars, and as we circled the lot, a gentleman waved at us to stop. He pointed to his RV and told us they were leaving and would rather give us the spot than have it be taken by another car. Once again, a reminder to avoid arriving on a weekend.

Although we'd not had a cell signal for most of the day, Kait was able to get one and looked up a few dispersed camping areas outside of the park. I had my doubts since we weren't successful in finding a suitable one in Moab, but I figured it was worth a shot.

"Why don't I take the Jeep and go scout a few of the roads," Kait suggested. "In twenty minutes, you leave with the motorhome and drive down 64. I'll take a walkie-talkie, and just radio me when you're getting close since we probably won't have cell coverage out there. If we can't find anything, we'll just keep driving to Flagstaff. There's a Walmart there we can spend the night at, but it's about a two-hour drive."

Twenty minutes later I spotted the Jeep parked along the side of 64 at the entrance to a Forest Road in the Kaibab National Forest. Over the radio Kait assured me the road was in great shape and she'd found the perfect spot for us. When I drove in with the motorhome, I saw how right she was. The site was a large, flat, open area in the middle of the forest. Someone had built a fire ring out of stones, and there wasn't another camper around.

It's just after seven and with coffee in hand, I'm standing outside surveying our campsite. I normally don't wake up this early, but it feels natural in the middle of the forest. There's dew on the grass and the morning sun's rays are just beginning to shine through the canopy of pine. Fall is upon us, but while leaves elsewhere are beginning to change color, the forest here will remain green all season long.

It's quite cold this morning. The thermostat informed me that it was only fifty-two in the motorhome and feels much colder out here. Leo was curled up on his bed, and when I stepped outside, he gave no indication that he'd be up anytime soon.

We have two folding chairs set up outside and, wiping the dew off of one, I sit down and chuckle to myself. These are the same chairs we had set up as temporary living room furniture when we first moved into our house, and now here they are in this amazing area. It's completely tranquil and so far from the life of the concrete jungle we left behind. Seeing the crowds yesterday reminded me that people come out here to escape city life. We can stay out here and don't have to worry about going back to reality on Monday morning. This is reality. This is our new normal.

As much as I would like to say we could park our butts out here indefinitely, we're limited on how long we can stay. The first limitation is our holding tanks. Once they're full or we run out of water, it's time for us to leave. Even if we can hold out, this area of dispersed camping has a fourteen-day limit.

The other limitation is our batteries. Before we left, I installed two deep-cycle six-volt golf cart batteries in the motorhome. With our one-hundred-watt portable solar panel, we've found that if we're conservative, the batteries will last about a day. If we don't have enough sun for the solar panel, then we have to run the onboard generator to recharge them. Well, one of the few downsides of being in the middle of the forest is that there is very little sunlight that makes it through the canopy. This means we'll be running the generator regularly if we want to stay out here for any length of time. While easy to do, the generator is loud and disruptive to anyone in earshot trying to enjoy the peace and quiet I am savoring at the moment.

Kait comes out and sits next to me. Leo is still asleep which is no surprise because he has never been a morning dog. After enjoying the peace and quiet for a while, we discuss our plans for the day and decide to head into town to find a place with Wi-Fi to work for a few hours before heading into the park.

"Look!" Kait yells. Her excitement startles the pronghorn she's spotted and it goes bounding through the forest.

"Beautiful. Next time don't scare it away," I say with a laugh. "How about I make us some breakfast, and then we can head into town."

Breakfast consists of leftover chili, which I throw in a skillet and fry with eggs. Growing up, my father and I would always fry up whatever leftovers were in the fridge with eggs and this breakfast makes me think of him. If he were still alive I think he'd love to join us out here. I would call my mom and invite her, but her idea of roughing it is a Motel 6.

"We're running low on food," I tell Kait, setting a plate of chili and eggs in front of her with a fresh cup of coffee. "This was the last of our eggs."

"We can check out the general store when we go into the park today," Kait suggests. "I know they sell food there."

Before leaving the motorhome, we take a quick inventory of what food we have. There's a package of brats in the freezer along with a bag of mixed veggies, a couple cans of tomato sauce, a bag of brown rice, a bag of chicharrones we picked up at a gas station and about five cans of Spam. Since Spam lasts for years, it was part of our emergency earthquake supplies in California, which we've been slowly eating our way through.

Driving into town we begin looking for a place to call our office for the next few hours. To call Tusayan a town is a bit of a stretch. It's set up to cater to all of the park visitors and is mostly a collection of lodging and fast-food restaurants. As we roll through town, I see a large sign on the McDonald's advertising free Wi-Fi.

"How does McDonald's sound to you?" I ask Kait. "I can get a coffee there so we can use the Wi-Fi."

"I'm good with it."

When we arrive at the McDonald's, we find a booth next to the door with an outlet and set up shop. The Wi-Fi here is extremely slow. It reminds me of the days of dial-up, and simple updates to our website are taking forever. The cell coverage is minimal too so we're not able to tether with our phones instead of using Wi-Fi to get online. It's a reminder that working on the road is not always going to be easy and we need to remember that when we come to places like these, we may not have internet access. We've also discussed getting more cellular data added to our plan so we don't have to find a place to work when we do have cell coverage.

After a few hours, we're able to get a couple articles written and scheduled on the website, then leave for the park. Driving toward the main gate, the traffic comes to a stop almost a quarter mile from the entrance. After a moment of confusion as to why there is so much traffic, we realize it's Sunday and spend the next hour in line.

At the gate we decide to purchase the National Park Annual Pass. It's a steal at $80 considering all of the parks we plan to see along our journey, and it will make Kait happy every time we go in one because she'll know we're saving money.

"Leo, are you ready to see the Grand Canyon?" Kait asks after we find a spot to park.

"Oh, I think he is," I say as Leo starts spinning around in circles in the back of the Jeep.

Walking along the rim, I am overwhelmed by the sight of the canyon. Leo loves it here and is walking like he's on a mission to circle the entire Grand Canyon. Being a Siberian husky, he goes into work mode whenever we're on a trail. He's not veering from the path and is so focused that he doesn't seem to care about the groups of tourists meandering ahead of us.

"Excuse me...sorry...excuse us...sorry about that," I say as Leo threads his way through groups of people.

"AAAAHHHH!" A Chinese woman screams as she looks down to find Leo brushing past her leg. She's so afraid that she grabs the man she's with and uses him as a shield. I'm not sure if it's Leo's size or his wolf-like resemblance, but something about him has her afraid for her life. "Sorry," I say again.

This scene is repeated numerous times on our walk before we reach the Grand Canyon general store. "I want to go in and see what they have," Kait says. "I don't know how many days in a row I can eat Spam."

As we're waiting outside, Leo and I see quite a few campers walking out with full grocery bags heading back to Mather Campground. When Kait walks out, all she has is a bag of potato chips.

"What happened?" I ask.

"Everything in there is so expensive. They wanted $16.99 per pound for a steak that didn't look very good. Let's try to eat everything we have in the motorhome before we buy anything else. At these prices, I want to only buy something if it's absolutely necessary."

I nod my head at the bag of chips and ask, "Necessity?"

"I'm hungry so I got the chips for us to snack on," Kait says with a smile.

"How much were the chips?"

"$5."

"Wow, steaks aren't the only expensive thing in there. I knew we should have gone shopping before we drove down here. I bet the next real grocery store is in Flagstaff."

"You were right. Lesson learned: stock up on food before we come out to a remote place like this."

We continue our walk along the rim. It's getting close to sunset, so the three of us find a spot on one of the points along the rim to sit and watch the sun set behind the Grand Canyon. As much as I am enjoying sitting there with Kait and Leo, I can't stop thinking about Duke. I wish he were here with us, getting to experience the Grand Canyon. It might get easier over time, but I'll always miss having him by my side.

When we get back to the campground, I spend half an hour walking around our campsite picking up dead wood for a campfire. Every time I stop, I can't get over just how quiet it is here. We're only about a half mile from the main road, but all I can hear is the wind through the pines. This is the first time we've been able to find a dispersed camping spot that could accommodate our motorhome, and I'm hoping we find many more in the future.

"The fire's ready," I say, popping my head into the motorhome. "I'll bring the chairs over if you want to grab the bag of chicharrones. Oh, and don't let me forget, there's something I want to burn when you come out here."

"Do you want a beer to go with the chicharrones?"

"You read my mind; I'd love one."

Sitting next to the fire with my beer and chicharrones, looking out through the forest, I realize that this is what I had imagined when we talked about this lifestyle. I feel at peace here. That is until I look down and see Leo staring back at me.

"Okay, you can have one," I say to a very eager Leo. Reaching into the bag, I grab one of the larger pieces of fried pig skin and hold it out to Leo.

"Sit." Leo drops his butt to the ground and is laser focused on the fried pork resting between my fingers. Unlike Duke, Leo will not listen to commands unless you have something he wants, so I savor this moment before giving him the treat. When I finally hand it to him, he snatches it out of my hand and walks away to enjoy it in peace.

"One day you're going to lose a finger," Kait says with a sideways smile.

We had a great time today hiking the rim with Leo and I suggest going back one of these days to watch the sun rise and do some more hiking. Kait nods her head in agreement and after a moment asks, "Wasn't there something you were going to burn?"

"I almost forgot!" I exclaim, getting up and going inside the motorhome. It takes me a few minutes to find it, but back outside, I hold up what I am about to toss in.

"You're going to burn your ten-year plaque?" Kait asks.

"Yep. After the talk we had a few days ago, I'm really motivated to make this life work. I want to burn this because it signifies a life that I don't ever want to go back to. The only thing I regret about what we're doing is that we didn't do it sooner," I say, tossing the plaque into the fire. Turning towards Kait, I hold my beer up, "To a new chapter!"

There is enough dead wood scattered around our site to keep the fire going all night but around nine p.m., we decide to call it a night and head back inside the motorhome. The temperature has dropped outside, and it's supposed to be in the low forties. Although it's still comfortable inside the motorhome, we grab a few extra blankets to toss on the bed. It hasn't been cold enough to run the heat and Leo seems quite happy with the cooler temperature.

Tuesday, October 13th, 2015

Holding up my phone, I look at the time: 4:32 a.m. "Seriously?" I mumble to myself.

"What's that noise?" Kait says coming out of a deep sleep.

"That is the elks bugling. Apparently they like to start around 4:30 in the morning. So much for sleeping in."

After lying in bed for a bit we decide to take advantage of the wake-up call and head into the park to watch the sun rise. It's even more incredible than the sunset last night and something no one should miss. Afterwards, we stop by the registration office for Mather Campground and as luck would have it, they have a couple last minute cancelations and we book two nights of camping.

"I'm excited to camp in the park tomorrow," Kait says on our drive back to our dispersed camping spot.

"So am I. I'm enjoying the park and it would be nice not to have to deal with waiting in line to get in, parking and then driving back."

When we turn onto our forest road, we see the motorhome in the distance and both say, "Looks like it's still there."

Leaving our home behind in the middle of the forest is nerve racking for us because at least when we left it at a Walmart or Cracker Barrel, there were people around. Almost everything we own is in there and it's a bit odd just leaving it in the middle of a forest with no one around. Aside from the two locks on the door, we don't have any other way to protect the motorhome from being broken into. Sure, we've seen a few other campers, but no one would notice if someone was breaking into our motorhome. Even if they did notice, the robbers would be long gone before the police had time to make it out here, assuming the person who spotted them had a cell signal.

The rest of the evening is spent working on the website. Although we can't get on the internet, we both write posts on our computers that we can upload when we get Wi-Fi. We've decided to try and publish three articles a week. I can already tell the schedule we set is going to be taxing on us with all of the travel and sightseeing we're doing.

Honey, what's that noise?" Kait asks, nudging me to wake up.

"Uh, it sounds like a car just pulled up," I respond and get out of bed to investigate.

Opening one of the shades, I see a car parked about five feet from our motorhome. While this isn't something I would normally worry about if we were parked at a Walmart, we're in the middle of the forest and aside from us and whoever is in that car, we're all alone out here with no cell signal to call for help.

From my vantage point at the window, I explain the situation to Kait, who's now sitting up in bed. "I can't see how many people are in the car but someone just got out and is looking around our motorhome."

"What should we do?" Kait asks with nervousness in her voice.

"Let's wait a minute and see what happens."

The person continues to walk around our campsite, moving farther away from the motorhome. After a few minutes, they get back in their car and park it near the edge of our camp site.

"It looks like they were just scouting for a place to park. They moved to the opposite side of the site and might be camping here tonight."

Watching our new neighbors, I see them begin to unpack their car and get a fire started.

"There are so many other spots out here, why'd they park here?" Kait asks.

"I don't know, but let's get some sleep."

The next morning, we're woken up by large trucks driving along the forest road. It's unusual because, aside from the odd camper or pickup, there has been very little traffic. Our new neighbors have started a fire for breakfast and by the looks of it, plan to stay a few nights.

"Good thing we're leaving today," Kait says.

"Agreed. It will be nice to stay in the park for a few nights."

It doesn't take us long to pack up, and instead of hooking up the Jeep, we decide to drive separately to the campground. When we arrive, I see that Mather Campground is set up the same way Desert View is. The sites are all arranged in loops, and most are drive-through with a few back-in sites. All of the sites are dry with no electric hookups, water or sewer connections. There is a dump station and water fill near the entrance. We're basically paying $18 a night for a parking spot, fire ring and picnic table, but it's gorgeous here, and we're walking distance to the general store and rim of the canyon.

They assign us site 188 and it's not far from the start of our loop. Luckily, this campground seems like they've trimmed the trees a bit better and I have no issue driving to our site. After parking and setting up the motorhome, we walk over to the general store. Aside from a few cans of Spam, we've made it through most of the food we had left so it's time to stock up. Although the food at the general store is expensive, we'll save money not going out to eat. Since Leo has plenty of food, he decides to hang out in the motorhome so we can both go into the store to look around.

The general store is about the size of a standard grocery store. The right side is a giant gift shop selling all sorts of Grand Canyon memorabilia, hiking equipment and clothes. There is a small restaurant on the left side of the store serving burgers, hot dogs and things like that. The rest of the store is dedicated to groceries with fresh produce, meat, fish and lots of packaged goods.

Thirty-three dollars later, we're back at camp with a dozen eggs, a large slab of ham and a pound of red potatoes.

"If you set up the table and our camp stove, I'll make us brunch," Kait says.

"Absolutely, I'm starving. What do you need me to do besides setting up?"

"Nothing. Just sit, relax and keep me company. Maybe make yourself a cup of coffee?"

Kait loves to cook, and I can tell she's enjoying herself. She picked a nice spot in the shade for me to set up our folding table and the camp stove her parents gave us. From what she tells me, that stove has been around since her childhood and was part of the many camping adventures her parents took her on. She used to love sitting outside and cooking a meal on that stove, and I can see how much she's enjoying it now.

Brunch is wonderful, and afterwards we take Leo for a walk around the campground. It's fun to walk around and see everyone's setup. There are quite a few people tent camping, others in trailers, motorhomes and just about everything you can imagine. One person even has a wooden, homebuilt camper that looks pretty interesting.

We seem to notice the camper vans more than anything. When we were at the vineyard in Paso Robles, we met a woman who was staying there in her van. She had been living out of it for almost a year, and it had everything she needed. A bed, tiny bathroom, table and a little kitchen. We both agreed we could never live in something that small, but it was intriguing that this woman could park her van just about anywhere.

Most of the vans we see at the campground have been converted by different companies. However a few look like they're homebuilt. One couple had the side door open, and all they had inside was a blow-up mattress and sleeping bags.

"Honey, look," Kait whispers.

Looking up I see a family of elk about twenty-five yards ahead of us walking through the trees, investigating people's campsites. Kait stands and stares while Leo tries dragging me towards them. He's not aggressive, just curious to find out what the giant animals are.

When we get back to the motorhome, I make a pot of coffee and kick back with my laptop to try and write a few posts that we can upload later. "Looks like we have some neighbors," I say, pointing out the window at the family who's just pulled into the spot across from us in a rental RV.

Our new neighbors spend quite a bit of time unpacking, and we're amazed at how much stuff they brought with them. They have bikes, chairs, tables, a BBQ and quite a few other things. All we have set up is a folding table and two chairs. Watching this unfold I think about how much we've simplified our lives, realizing we don't need so many things. It's refreshing that when we leave in a few days, we won't have to spend hours packing up.

"That's weird," I say, looking back out the window. "Another RV just pulled into the site where the rental is parked."

"What do you mean?" Kait asks, looking up from her laptop.

"Well, this other family pulled up with their trailer into the spot where the rental is set up. The guy with the trailer seems pretty upset. I'm guessing the people in the rental may have parked in the wrong spot."

The newcomer is showing his registration form to the woman in the rental. I can hear her telling the guy that he's going to have to talk to her husband, who's not there at the moment. He tells the woman that he's going back to the registration office to have them look into this and drives off.

Our neighbor looks a bit concerned, and when her husband returns a few minutes later, they start throwing everything into their rental and drive off.

"I wonder what happened," Kait says.

"My guess is that they didn't have a reservation and took a chance on a vacant spot."

"I haven't seen the rangers checking campsites at night, only during the day," Kait says. "Who knew staying at a campground could be so eventful?"

Our new neighbors return about fifteen minutes later and get their campsite set up. They too have quite a bit of stuff, but it looks like they also have five kids, some of which are currently setting up a tent for themselves. Smart, I think. Let the kids sleep in the tent while the adults get some privacy in the camper.

The next morning we head out for another walk around the park with Leo, stopping at the registration booth to see if we can snag another last-minute reservation. Unfortunately nothing is available, so we head back to the motorhome and make plans to head to Sedona via Flagstaff tomorrow. It's supposed to start raining this afternoon so we decide to put our table and chairs away and spend the rest of the day inside working and reading.

That night as we're laying in bed, the rain starts coming down pretty hard. It's a much different experience to be in the rain in a motorhome than a house or an apartment because you can hear every drop hitting the roof. It makes us realize how little is between us and what's outside. Since Leo doesn't like going out in the rain, it's nice that we can put the awning out to keep the rain off of him when he needs to relieve himself.

BONUS CONTENT: Curious about our free camping spot outside the National Park? Here it is: https://weretherussos.com/free-camping-outside-grand-canyon-south-rim/

10. OUR FAVORITE CITY

Saturday, October 17th, 2015

We would have liked to have stayed at the campground until Monday and not travel on the weekend, but since there was no availability, we packed up and left the park. We took State Route 64 from the park south towards Williams and then got on Interstate 40 towards Flagstaff or "Flag," as the locals call it. We needed gas so once we had cell signal again, Kait pulled up the Gas Buddy app and found a Pilot truck stop outside of town that had the lowest prices. When we pulled in, I saw a sign for a CAT Scale. These are the scales truckers use to weigh their loads. I was interested because we have been worried about whether or not we overloaded our motorhome.

Every RV comes with a sticker displaying the unladen vehicle weight (UVW) of the unit as built and then the occupant and cargo carrying capacity (OCCC) which is the combined weight of occupants, cargo and a full tank of water that you can safely carry. We specifically bought this motorhome because it had a much higher OCCC than most of the other units we saw in the same size due to its 22,000 pound gross vehicle weight rating (GVWR) chassis. If a vehicle exceeds the GVWR, then there can be some possible safety issues like overloading the tires which can lead to a blowout.

After I filled the gas tank, we decided to get the motorhome weighed. The holding tanks were empty; I dumped them before leaving the campground and filled up on water, which meant we would get an accurate idea of whether we were under or overweight. I drove the motorhome, with Jeep in tow, around back and up onto the scale. The weigh-in was simple. Once I pulled forward, I pressed the intercom button and told the person who answered that I was there to be weighed. By the time Kait walked inside and paid the $10 fee, they had a printout for her with our weight for the front and rear axles along with the trailer weight—the trailer being our Jeep. We came in 2,000 pounds underweight, alleviating the concerns we had. There is another system called SmartWeigh that the Escapees RV Club uses which takes a measurement from under each tire. This way you not only know your RV's weight, but also how well the RV is balanced. We may do this in the future, but for now we're content to know we're well under the max weight of our motorhome.

Since we only plan to stop in Flagstaff for the night and continue south to Sedona, Kait finds a Cracker Barrel that allows overnight RV parking. After we got parked, we took the Jeep around to get a feel for the city and do some grocery shopping. Flagstaff is located 7,000 feet above sea level. I, like most people I know, always pictured Arizona as a huge desert full of cacti and scrub pines, but most of northern Arizona is forest, especially around Flagstaff.

"Look honey, there's snow on the mountains," Kait says, as we were driving towards downtown. "Maybe we can take Leo up there before we leave tomorrow; he's never been in snow."

"I didn't expect to see snow in Arizona, especially in October."

As we drive around, Kait mentions that there is a couple she follows on Instagram who are in Flagstaff and asks if we should try meeting up with them. I thought it would be fun and told Kait to send them a message. They quickly got back to us, and we made plans to meet tomorrow for coffee.

Driving through the historic downtown, Kait and I are amazed at how vibrant the area is. Everyone seems to be out walking and going out for the evening. With the university within walking distance, there seem to be a lot of college kids out as well.

"I'd love to get out and walk around, but I'm starving," I tell Kait.

"Me too. I saw there's a Whole Foods in town. Why don't we go there and pick something up for dinner? We can explore more tomorrow."

Going to the grocery store is never a good idea when you're hungry. Everything looked delicious, and after a brief deliberation, I buy a huge porterhouse steak for Kait and me to share and get some onions and peppers to sauté with it. The bill is more than we'd like to spend, and we'll have to find some way to offset it by cutting back somewhere else if we plan to keep our expenses down this month. Kait jokes that it would have been less expensive if we'd eaten dinner at Cracker Barrel than gone shopping.

Ever since we hit the road, Kait's been keeping track of our expenses. Last month, on average, we spent $127.60 per day. This includes everything - food, gas, insurance, registration, RV payment, cell phones, etc. Our goal for this month is to get our daily expenses under $100, and so far we've been doing a great job. With every dollar we save, it means we can stay on the road that much longer and an expensive meal or night on the town is one less day on the road. That realization completely changed how we see expenditures, and we've made it our mission to cut as much of our spending as we can while still enjoying ourselves. We decided to share our monthly expense reports on our website (https://weretherussos.com/rv-living-costs-full-time-class-a-motorhome/) to help keep track and to serve as a point of reference for other people looking to do the same thing.

While many people might cherish sleeping out in the forest, I find myself waking up in the Cracker Barrel parking lot feeling totally rested. Getting out of bed, I ask, "What time are we meeting Dan and Kathy?"

"Good morning, sleepy head."

"Are you talking to me or Leo?" I ask, pointing to our boy still passed out on his bed.

Kait gives me one of her looks and says, "We're meeting them at eleven. But before we meet them, I was thinking that we could go scope out a few dispersed camping spots after breakfast."

"Do I have time to make coffee?"

"We're getting coffee with the Kelleys; can't you wait?"

"You're being sarcastic, right?"

"Oh boy. Leo, somebody has a problem!" Kait says. "Can you at least put some clothes on before you make your coffee. I don't want you burning anything off."

I oblige and get dressed before I start the water for my coffee. Firing up our propane stove, I pour a bottle of water into my small gooseneck kettle and set it on the burner. Opening the pantry, I grab my automatic burr grinder along with my pour over and a filter. I have the pour over for days like these when I just want a single cup. I also have a four cup Chemex for those other times I want a "pot" or when Kait wants to join me for a cup.

After Kait gets her fill of hash-brown casserole at Cracker Barrel, we decide to move the motorhome over to Walmart for the day. The number of RVs in the lot there seems to have grown since we drove past last night and we have a tough time finding a place to park. A majority of the RVs at the back of the lot are old, beaten up motorhomes and trailers. I question whether some will even run. One Class C RV looks like the entire rear end was in a bad collision and is now being held in place by a number of ratchet straps and duct tape. Some of the people here are living out of their RVs out of necessity rather than by choice. I also see a lot of people who seem to be drifters hanging around the lot with backpacks and sleeping rolls. That said, there are an equal number of well-cared-for RVs and people who look like they are enjoying retirement.

Our scouting trip in the Jeep turns out to be a bust. We found some areas for camping with decent roads, but there is rain on the forecast, and I was worried that area would become muddy and increase the chances of our motorhome getting stuck. As much as I love the space we have in our motorhome, something smaller with four-wheel drive would give us access to many more places.

Although we didn't find a place to camp, we did find some snow. We've watched videos of huskies playing and jumping in the snow and we figured snow to them was like water to labs. Apparently Leo didn't get that memo because he seemed completely unimpressed with the white stuff.

Driving into Flagstaff, we pass back through the historic downtown area. This town grew up around the railroad which splits the historic section. "I'd really like to walk around here after we meet the Kelleys," Kait says while we are waiting at the railroad crossing for a long freight train to pass.

Dan and Kathy arrive at the cafe shortly after us, and we all grab a table outside so Leo can join us.

We spend almost two hours talking to Dan and Kathy. They were in the same position we were before deciding to hit the road. Full-time careers which left little time for life. In contrast to us, they really enjoyed what they did and were able to convince their employers to let them work remotely. Now they travel full-time in a large tow-behind trailer. Most of the camping they do is dispersed, rarely spending time at campgrounds. They gave us advice on how to find good spots and some apps to download that would help point us in the right direction. They even invite us to camp with them at their dispersed camping spot. It was refreshing to sit down and talk to a couple who understood us and our new lifestyle.

After we say our goodbyes, we take Leo for a walk around town. The city has a lot to offer. A couple micro breweries, a diverse selection of restaurants and all sorts of local shops. Although we really don't buy things anymore, it's still enjoyable to walk in and look. Plus most shops allow Leo to come in with us. Based on our research, Flagstaff is supposed to be a dog friendly city, and so far it's true.

"I'm really enjoying Flagstaff," Kait says. "Are you interested in staying a bit longer if we can camp with the Kelleys?

"Absolutely, but let's take the Jeep down there tomorrow and scope it out. I don't want to drive the motorhome down a dirt road we haven't scouted yet."

"I hope we can camp out there," Kait says. "There are a few national parks close to here that I'd love to visit."

"The nice thing about not having reservations is we don't have to be in Sedona at any specific time," I respond.

The next morning we take the Jeep and head out to find Dan and Kathy's camping spot. The road to their campsite is one of the best maintained Forest Service roads we've seen. There are camping spots all along the road, but most are occupied. About a half mile off the main road, we spot their trailer parked in a large open area that sits about a hundred yards from the road. The established campsite looks big enough to fit ten motorhomes. I can see why they love this spot so much.

As nice as the site is, I noticed an issue right away. A small wash between the road and the entrance to the site. It's only a foot or two deep, and while we'd have no problem crossing it in the Jeep, the motorhome might be another story. With the rear overhang, I'm afraid we'd bottom out and possibly get stuck. I'm also concerned because it's going to rain and even if we do make it in, a heavy rain could make the wash more difficult to cross on the way out.

We continued driving down the road and spotted a number of other sites. Some would be a challenge accessing with the Jeep, impossible in the motorhome. Eventually we found one that had good access and a nice view. The site is fairly level and located next to a large open field where some cows are grazing. On our way back, Kait asks if I want to stop at the Kelleys' and hang out for a bit.

"Let's head back and get the motorhome," I say to Kait. "I'm worried that by the time we get back here, the site will be gone. These are all first come, first served, and there's no way to save the spot."

"I think we'll be fine but if you'd feel better getting the motorhome before we go see the Kelleys, I'm good with that."

"Thanks. It's a forty-minute round trip, and I've seen a few other people driving down this road looking for spots."

An hour later we're back and Kait was right, no one took the spot. However I notice another problem. There's a small ditch running along the entrance to the site and it will be more difficult to get into the site than expected. I decide to try crossing the ditch at an angle. Kait goes outside with her radio to act as my spotter, giving me updates and suggestions on how to best get through as I creep along. Despite the rear overhang of the motorhome getting dangerously close to the ground, we make it in with no problems.

Once we were parked, we realized the site was much more off-level than it first looked. If the motorhome is too off-level, it could affect the operation of the slides and the propane fridge which has to be within a few degrees of level to work properly. On my first attempt to level with the hydraulic jacks, I hit the limit of their extension. The front wheels were off the ground and we still weren't level. To fix that, I retracted the jacks and had Kait place leveling blocks in front of the two front wheels. She added an extra layer on the right side since there was a bit of a slope. When they were in place, I drove the motorhome slowly onto the blocks, stopping when Kait gave the signal that the wheels were in the right spot. She then placed blocks under the jacks. At this point, the motorhome was almost level and I didn't need to raise the motorhome much with the jacks to finish the job.

After we got set up, we took Leo for a walk to explore and fell in love with the area. It is so quiet and peaceful that we forgot there was a city a few miles away. We can see a few other campers in the area, but aside from the occasional freight train blowing its horn in the distance, the only noise we heard was the breeze through the trees. Once it got dark, the stars came out, and we just stood together and were in awe of how the stars lit up the sky in the absence of light pollution. After our experience in the forest outside of the Grand Canyon and now Flagstaff, we are hooked on dispersed camping.

Before we embraced RV life, I had no idea what dispersed camping or boondocking was. Boondocking is the act of camping without any hookups. It can be in a Walmart parking lot or in the middle of the forest. Dispersed camping is the term for boondocking on Forest Service or Bureau of Land Management (BLM) land. The couple times we've gone into a ranger station and asked about camping, we specifically ask where we're allowed to disperse camp. So far the rangers have been very helpful, providing maps and even telling us about things to watch out for or go check out.

Our one night in Flagstaff quickly turned into multiple, and on our fourth night in the Coconino National Forest, we got woken up by an amazing lightning storm and pouring rain. Kait decided to check the weather app on her phone and got a bit nervous because temperatures were expected to drop below freezing that night. The concern was that our water lines would freeze and possibly burst. She called Newmar when they opened that morning and relayed her concerns to the customer service department. The gentleman from Newmar had a good laugh. "Miss, we have customers up in Minnesota right now in a few feet of snow. You'll be fine if it gets below freezing at night. If it doesn't get above freezing during the day, then you'll need to run the furnace which is ducted into the bays and will keep everything from freezing. But don't worry; you won't have a problem."

While we didn't have to worry about freezing, we did have to worry about sinking. I'd noticed that we were beginning to get a bit off-level, and when I went outside to investigate, I found that with all of the rain, the leveling blocks we put under the wheels and jacks were sinking into the mud. We'd used all of our blocks and didn't have anything else to put under the wheels, so I decided to just let the motorhome be. I was afraid that if we tried moving the motorhome the wheels would sink into the mud. Since there was nothing we could do, we drove into town to find a place with Wi-Fi where we could get some work done.

I'm starting to get back into the swing of working and putting in time on the website. We have a very weak signal at our campsite, so we found a small cafe in town that allows dogs inside, makes a cup of great coffee and a spicy chai latte that is worth every calorie.

We spend some time each day at the cafe, working on updates and articles for the website before exploring more of the area. One day when I walked up to order my coffee, the girl at the register recognized me from our daily visits and told me how the staff had been admiring Leo. I thanked her for allowing him inside since we'd run across places that wouldn't let dogs in because it might upset other people. Her response to me was that if someone complained about the dogs, they'd be asked to leave. Dogs were very much welcomed at this cafe.

We've found that by getting out of the motorhome and going to a cafe, we can get a lot more work done because we're more focused. Each day we set office hours. It differs depending on what we have to work on but when we are at the cafe, we are working. With the consistent posts to our website, we are beginning to see an increasing number of people reading and commenting. Every morning we check our analytics and get excited when we see that ten or fifteen people checked out the site the day before. We get ecstatic when someone leaves a comment asking a question and may spend up to thirty minutes writing a detailed response.

It feels great to be back on the same page and working as a team. We stopped arguing about the little stuff and don't get on each other's nerves. We know that if we work together, we have a real shot at growing our website and turning this lifestyle into something that can support us. That said, the chances of building the website to a point where it can cover all our expenses are slim. Expenses this month will be close to $3,000, and we are barely making enough on the website to buy a cup of coffee. When we project how much we need to grow in order to cover our expenses, it seems impossible. Few blogs become that big, and even if they do, it takes years of work. We don't have years, so Kait has been talking again about finding a remote work position while I spend the bulk of my time on the site in hopes that we can eventually grow it.

"Don't worry; I'll be your sugar momma," she says every time I ask about the jobs she's looking at. More and more tech companies these days are hiring people to work remotely. The types of jobs vary, but she's looking into becoming a "Happiness Consultant," or something like that. The way she explains, it's a creative name for a customer support agent.

I'm still opposed to the idea of Kait working until we absolutely need the money. That first Friday we were on the road and no paycheck was deposited was a dose of reality for both of us. Even though we've only been on the road for a month and a half, we're starting to feel the pressure of watching our account slowly dwindle. More than anything, we just want to find a way to keep going.

Although we aren't making anything significant off the website yet, the harder we work, the less concerned we are about our finances. It's the mentality that if we put in the effort, eventually it will pay off. However, we have decided that while we want to grow our business, we need to remember why we're doing this: to spend time with each other and see the world. We can't fulfill the latter if we're constantly staring at a computer screen, so after spending a few days of solid work at the cafe, some downtime is in order.

Our first day off was spent at Sunset Crater which is on the outskirts of Flagstaff. Around 1085 AD, there was a large eruption that created the crater, changing the surrounding landscape forever. Unfortunately they don't allow people to walk inside the crater anymore, but you can see it from a distance. What I found more exciting was the narrow trail you can take through the lava fields. When you step onto the trail, you're transported to a prehistoric landscape that makes you feel like you're on another planet.

After the park we headed back into downtown Flagstaff. On our way through the center of town, we stumbled across a Northern Arizona University pep rally. The square was packed with people. Kait walked around to check out the different booths they had set up, and Leo and I stood off to the side. That is, until one of the NAU cheerleaders spotted Leo and the entire squad descended on us. When Kait walked back over, I said, "I should have had Leo when I was single." She just laughed and walked away to let her boys enjoy the attention.

It was dusk when we got back to the area where we were camped. Driving along the main road, we saw a family of deer cross about a hundred yards ahead of us. Kait got excited, and then we saw a cougar following their trail. It was stalking the family, and I figured one of the fawns wouldn't be making it home that night.

The next morning, we drove to Petrified Forest National Park, about 110 miles east of Flagstaff. We arrived around noon and spent four hours driving through the park. We were both in awe of all the "trees" scattered throughout the area. Each time we stopped at a pullout, there was another beautiful scene dotted with all of these petrified trees. The landscape was surreal, and it has become one of Kait's favorite national parks.

Monday, October 26th, 2015

After nine days of being camped outside of Flagstaff, our forty-gallon black tank was showing three-quarters full, so we decided it was time to find a dump station and make our way south to Sedona. Our new friends, Dan and Kathy, left almost a week ago heading east and we made a promise to them that when we cross paths again, we do some more camping together.

There hasn't been any more rain in the last few days so the ground is firm again, alleviating my concerns of the motorhome getting stuck. When I backed the motorhome off the leveling blocks this morning, we just had to dig them out of the now dry mud. Good thing we keep a small shovel on board.

Kait found a free dump station at one of the gas stations in town, so we stopped there on our way south. Back in Los Angeles, it cost us $30 each time we wanted to dump. When we calculated our budget for the year, we anticipated having to pay quite a bit to use dump stations, but Kait has been able to find plenty of free ones. Forty-four days on the road and we haven't paid a penny to dump the tanks, with the exception of the campgrounds we've stayed at where it was included with our stay.

At the gas station, while I was waiting for the tanks to finish emptying, I performed a walk-around of the motorhome and Jeep, checking tire pressures and making sure everything was in order. When I got to the Jeep, I noticed a large nail buried in one of the tires. The tire hadn't lost any pressure and I briefly considered continuing to Sedona before changing it, but I decided I don't want to run the risk of blowing a tire while towing. Once the tanks were empty and I topped off our water tank, we drove over to an adjacent parking lot where I put the spare on. Another reason I love the Jeep is the full-size spare rim and tire it has. We put together our checklist specifically for reasons like this (here's our checklist: https://weretherussos.com/rv-checklist-predeparture/)

Nine days. That's the longest we've stayed in any one place. I found that not having to constantly think about moving again was very relaxing and allowed me to enjoy the area. We also began to have our regular spots like the cafe. We'd go in, people would recognize Leo (not us) and it began to feel like we were back in our community. Flagstaff just felt relaxed and comfortable—like home—and has become our favorite city.

BONUS CONTENT: Want to know more about free camping on public land? Here's our guide to dispersed camping: https://weretherussos.com/free-camping-in-national-forests-dispersed-camping/

11. SEDONA

With the tire changed, we were ready to head to Sedona, Arizona. The question was, which route do we take? The thing we've learned about driving a vehicle that's this tall, wide and long with another vehicle in tow is, research the route and conditions before we get rolling. As much as we rely on the Garmin RV GPS, we've learned it's important to double check road conditions by asking fellow travelers or doing research on the internet. When we looked up the road to Sedona from Flagstaff, we had two main options: head south on 89A or Interstate 17.

We learned that 89A becomes a very tight, winding road in certain sections, and isn't recommend for large vehicles towing a trailer. Instead we took I-17, which is a longer but easier drive for our setup. The 17 put us south of Sedona, so we decided to swing by the ranger station to get a map and some suggestions of dispersed camping in the area. They pointed us to a few different locations they thought we could get our motorhome into and a couple to avoid. There are pockets of BLM land all around Sedona so we were excited to go and claim a spot for ourselves.

Most of the areas we drove to were either packed full of campers, or the roads were too rough for us to get in. After about an hour of searching, we found Forest Road 120. The dirt road leading to the site was tight with scrub brush on either side, but it was level and free of ruts. When we reached the site, we noticed that the dirt wasn't hard pack but rather very fine sand, almost like a dried river bed. Before parking,

I checked the compass on my phone to make sure the front of the RV was pointed south. Since the house batteries are located in the front of the RV, south is the optimal direction for setting up our 100 watt portable solar panel. As I was setting up the panel, I noticed that our camping spot wasn't as empty as we thought it was, but rather well inhabited by fire ants—something to remember when taking Leo out at night so we don't accidentally stand on one of their mounds. Regardless, we were happy we found this spot and ready to spend a week exploring Sedona.

Tuesday, October 26th, 2015

Opening the large front shade, the morning sun's rays are a welcome addition to the chilly interior of the motorhome. Before making my coffee, I go outside to reposition our solar panel towards the rising sun. The nice thing with having the portable unit is that we can move it throughout the day so it has optimal sunlight hitting it. When we go out for the day, I have a long bicycle chain that I can use to lock the panel to the motorhome so someone can't run off with it. Back inside, a quick check of our battery monitor reveals that the solar is doing its job, and the candles we used last night allowed us to conserve enough energy for me to turn on the inverter and grind my coffee beans.

Kait and I decide that after breakfast, we'll go into Sedona and walk Leo through the city. It looks like it's going to be a gorgeous day and perfect to do some sightseeing.

"I'm surprised it's this busy on a weekday," Kait says as we drive down another street in search of parking. "I'm glad we didn't try coming down here last weekend."

"Are we tourists if we're technically living out here?" I ask.

"Oh, interesting," Kait says as she ponders my question. "Since we're nomads now, I'd say that anywhere we go is home, and in this case, I would say we're locals, if only temporarily. Why do you ask?"

"Just something that popped in my head as we're driving through town."

What's locally known as the Uptown area of Sedona is a big tourist destination. The sidewalks of the main drag are filled with people. Most are browsing through shops displaying art from local artists, handmade jewelry and various Southwestern goods. Despite the chill in the air, we see many people walking with an ice cream cone in hand.

At the edge of Uptown, we manage to find a place to park. Leo certainly doesn't mind the walk, and we could both use the exercise. Kait and I join everyone else as we stroll along inspecting the shops. While Kait stops to look at the menu of a Mexican restaurant, Leo and I check out one of the local Jeep tours.

Looking down at a flyer, I hear, "Do you have a place to stay?"

"Kind of," I say, looking up at the guy behind the counter. "We're currently camped outside of town on BLM land."

"Oh, you're in an RV. Would you like a three night free stay at a local resort that has a small RV park?"

"What's the catch?" I ask suspiciously.

"The only catch is that you have to sit in on a ninety-minute time-share presentation. I take a $100 deposit here which you get back in full once you've finished the presentation."

After checking with Kait, we decide to do it. While we like our campsite, it would be nice after our time in Flagstaff to have full hookups and be able to take a real shower.

Later that day we check into the resort. Aside from the RV spots being a bit tight, it seems like a great place. Large lap pool, multiple Jacuzzis, gas BBQs and, best of all, free laundry. We haven't done laundry since we hit the road, and I'm almost at the point where I'm going to have to turn my underwear inside out so it can be worn again.

We learned another important lesson today. Don't rely on other people to guide you into an RV site. After check-in the resort had us follow a staff member to our site. Once there he began to guide me into the back-in site while Kait brought the Jeep around. Upon seeing the RV, Kait jumped out and started screaming for me to stop, but it was too late. I'd scraped the motorhome once again on a branch. I'd trusted the person who'd been guiding me to know what he was doing and what to look for, but that wasn't the case. Luckily, the offending branch didn't leave much of a mark.

The ninety-minute presentation we sat through for the timeshare the following morning was actually kind of interesting. The company has properties all around the world and the idea of being able to pick a location just about anywhere to spend a couple weeks definitely sounds appealing. When we leave, Kait and I both remark that if we can get our website earning enough money to continue traveling, then all we would need is an internet connection and we could go pretty much anywhere in the world as digital nomads.

TALES FROM THE OPEN ROAD

We spent the next few days exploring the area around Sedona and even venturing off to see the city of Jerome, a former mining town turned artist colony. We love the area, but the highlight of our time in Sedona was the Broken Arrow Trail. While I was checking out the various Jeep tours in the area, I saw one highlighted for the Broken Arrow Trail. After some research, we found that it's a moderately difficult three-and-a-half mile one-way loop. I was doubtful our stock Jeep Wrangler would make it until we spoke to a gentleman camped three sites over from us. He too has a Jeep and said we should have no problems as he takes his down the trail whenever he's in town. I've always wanted a Jeep and one of the reasons was to be able to take it on trails like this. Now that I knew the Jeep could tackle it, I was ready to show Kait why I wanted it in the first place.

There's a ledge at the start of the trail, and it's said that if your vehicle can make it up the ledge, then you'll be fine on the rest of the trail. Well, the Jeep had no problem, so we continued on. As the trail began to get more and more challenging, that initial ledge didn't seem to be much of a measuring stick. At different points our stock tires were spinning on the slick rock faces we were trying to climb, and Kait would have to get out to spot me. Each time we conquered an obstacle, Kait would smile and say, "This is so much better than the Indiana Jones ride at Disneyland!" Near the end of the loop, the last obstacle stood in front of us: The Devil's Staircase.

Stopped at the top of the Staircase looking down, I saw a steep series of slick rock steps and my heart began to race. From my vantage point, it seemed like one wrong move and you could either get stuck or roll over. Since this is a one-way trail, the only way out is down. Making sure the Jeep was in 4-low, I slowly eased the front wheels over the first ledge, keeping my foot on the brake. Kait had started walking down the Staircase as I began coming down the second ledge. Suddenly, the wheels began to slide down the rock despite the fact that I had my foot firmly on the brake. The Jeep slid down to the next step with a loud grinding sound as rock met the skid plates coming to an abrupt stop. Perched on the next step, the Jeep was angled so far forward that it felt like it could roll forward at any moment. A look of horror came across Kait's face, and she decided to climb out and walk the rest of the way down, acting as a spotter to make sure I had the best line. Leo was his usual self, relaxed and perched on the rear bench seat enjoying the ride.

The process repeated on each step. Ease forward with my foot firmly on the brake pedal until the Jeep began sliding down to the next step. Insert more grotesque sounds of rock grinding along skid plates. When I finally reached the bottom, a huge smile came across my face. Not only had we made it, but, aside from some scrapes on the skid plates, the Jeep was unharmed.

As we were driving out, Kait commented that she finally understood what off-roading really was. She had thought our forays onto dirt fire roads were true off-roading until she experienced this trail. She also now understood why I wanted a vehicle like this as a tow vehicle.

Sunday, November 1st, 2015

"I could definitely spend another few weeks here," Kait says as I pull the motorhome out of the resort and onto 89A headed south.

"Me too, but we need to keep moving if we plan to make it to Texas before the end of the year."

BONUS CONTENT: In an effort to create more content, I decided to mount a GoPro to the Jeep while we drove the Broken Arrow Trail. The video and more info on the Broken Arrow Trail can be found here: https://weretherussos.com/broken-arrow-trail-sedona-arizona/

12. BECOMING TEXANS

Monday, November 23rd, 2015

After spending a few more weeks in Arizona, we finally crossed into Texas, traveling along Interstate 10. The I-10 is a four-lane highway that cuts through the desert and is one of the main arteries for semi-trucks. If we weren't passing a truck, we were being passed by one. Every time a truck went by, the wind coming off it would try and push the motorhome off the road, causing whoever was driving to constantly work to keep the motorhome between the lines.

When we arrived in Texas, we were dreading not having the abundance of federal land available to camp on. Although Texas is the second largest state, only 1.5% of its land is owned by the federal government, and most of it is in the form of national parks and monuments with very little land available for camping. This means we were back to spending nights in Walmart and Cracker Barrel parking lots; a far cry from the serenity of our nights in the middle of a forest or desert. So after spending a couple days in parking lots around San Antonio, we decided to recharge a bit and stay at a real campground. They aren't our preferred place to camp, but we were ready for a break from conserving each drop of water and every watt of electricity. Every now and again it's nice to just turn all the lights on, run the water, not have to worry about where we're dumping our tanks next or have to listen to the generator recharging our batteries.

We'd heard good things about San Marcos, Texas, and Kait found a campground that had two nights available and booked it. We wanted to stay longer, but with Thanksgiving coming up, the park will be completely full for the holiday.

After getting set up at the campground, Kait and I went to take a long shower at the bath house. I got back before her and decided to take a cue from Leo, and lay down for a quick nap. As soon as I started dozing off, there was a frantic knock on the door.

"Hello! Hello! Are you home?" A woman yelled.

"Hold on a second; I'm coming!" I yelled back.

Opening the door I saw an elderly woman standing outside crying.

"Can I help you?" I asked.

"I'm so sorry to bother you, but my husband was just rushed to the hospital. He tripped and fell while he was walking into our RV and couldn't get up. They told me he's in the ICU, and I need to drive to the hospital. I knocked on all of my neighbors' doors but no one was willing to help."

"I'm so sorry to hear that. How can I help?"

"Well, I saw you with your dog, so I knew you were a dog person. I need someone who can watch our dog Daisy while I'm at the hospital. I can give you the keys to the RV, and she just needs to be walked and fed. Would you be able to do that?"

"I'd be happy to. Why don't I come over, meet Daisy, and you can show me where all her stuff is."

"Okay, thank you so much. No one else would help."

Grace and her husband just bought a new fifth wheel and hit the road a week ago. They'd always wanted to travel, and now in retirement, they want to spend their days seeing the country with their pup Daisy. Her husband has some health issues so they wanted to get on the road before he was no longer able to travel.

After a hurried tour of where Grace kept all of Daisy's food and notes on how often she needs to be walked, Grace hands me her only keys to their RV and speeds off.

"You'll never guess what happened," I say when Kait gets back from her shower. After telling her the story, she and I take Daisy and Leo for a walk. Daisy seems just as shaken up as Grace but we could tell that she was beginning to feel better with Leo around.

"Did she say how long she'd be at the hospital?" Kait asks as we circle the RV park.

"No, it didn't seem like she really knew what was going on and was anxious to get to the hospital. She did leave me her cell phone number, so I'll text her later if we don't hear anything."

A few hours later, we decided to check out a local brewery in the area. When we walked in, there were dogs running all over the place, a big table with food and a bunch of people having a good old time. When we walked up to the bar to order a couple beers, Kait asked if we could bring Leo inside. "Of course, all dogs are welcome here," a cheery bartender informed us.

I went out to grab Leo, and when I came back Kait was chatting with a woman. She and her husband were part owners of the brewery, and were hosting a "Friendsgiving" potluck. She insisted we join them and make ourselves a couple plates. There was a huge spread of food including some Louisiana inspired dishes. The beers were great but I kept getting up to go back and get more gumbo. I couldn't get enough of that stuff.

One thing we've found during our travels is how friendly and welcoming the people we've encountered have been. Something like this would be a rare occurrence in Los Angeles, but here in Texas it seems to be the norm. Leo has also become our ambassador because when people come over to meet him, we strike up a conversation.

We weren't the only ones making new friends. Leo had met a couple of the other dogs running around the place and was having a good time playing with them. We did keep him on a leash since huskies are notorious for being runners. When they get loose, they have a tendency to start running and might not stop for ten or twenty miles. Leo has gotten out a couple times in the past and lived up to the reputation. The last thing we wanted was someone opening a door and having Leo dart out between their legs.

We couldn't stay long because we wanted to get back and check on Daisy. Grace had texted me while we were at the bar to let me know she was planning on spending the night at the hospital. Her husband's condition was improving but he was still in ICU, and she didn't want to leave him.

The next day, after checking on Daisy, I texted Grace a photo of her pup so she knew everything was going well. I quickly got a text back letting me know her husband's condition had worsened significantly and she still had no idea when she'd be back. Her children were supposed to be flying in, and she asked if I could take care of Daisy until they arrived. I told her it wasn't a problem, but we'd be leaving the following day.

Shortly after dinner, I sent Grace another text to find out if anyone would be coming by to get her keys. I didn't get a response, so I went back over to check on Daisy. By this point Daisy had warmed up to me and was excited every time I opened the door. While I was taking her for a walk, my phone started vibrating. Pulling it out of my pocket I saw a text from Grace.

"Sorry for not getting back to you. My husband passed away this afternoon due to complications from his fall. Our kids are on their way and I'm waiting for them here. I don't know how to hook up the trailer, so my son is going to come by tomorrow and see if he can figure it out. Please leave the keys with the manager before you leave tomorrow and he'll pick them up."

I was stunned. Seven days into retirement, starting their dream life, Grace's husband had passed away. People had called us crazy for quitting our jobs and selling the house so we could live this life. To me, it was probably the sanest thing we'd ever done. After witnessing what Grace was going through, it reinforced the notion that anything could happen. Each day was precious, and we couldn't waste them sitting in an office all day. I was relieved because we'd made the choice to live our lives now rather than postponing it for a day that may never come. The only regret I have is that we didn't do it sooner. I never heard from Grace again, but I'll never forget that feeling I had when she told me her husband had passed away.

Wednesday, November 25th, 2015

Despite the Thanksgiving holiday, we were able to find another RV park in the area that had availability. When Kait had called to confirm our reservation, the manager told her that the park was still recovering from a flood a few months ago. When we arrived it looked like a bomb had gone off. There was debris everywhere. The ground, buildings and just about every other structure was covered with silt. The RVs at the park stuck out like sore thumbs; each one shiny and clean, in total contrast to everything around them.

During check-in we met the owner who told us that quite a few motorhomes had been washed away during the flood. The river the park is situated along flooded during the day while most people were out sightseeing. By the time people realized what was happening, roads into the area had been shut down and people couldn't get back to rescue their RVs.

Despite the cosmetic conditions, we have full hookups and a very welcoming staff. The park is also holding their annual Thanksgiving potluck tomorrow which we plan to attend. The only requirement is that we bring a side dish to go with the smoked turkeys and dessert the park was supplying.

"What's the name of the BBQ place around here?" I asked Kait after we got the motorhome set up in our site.

"Black's. Did you want to go?"

"I'd love to. We haven't had any good BBQ since we've been on the road, and we're in Texas."

"Let's do it, then. We need to go to the store anyway and figure out what we're going to do for a side dish."

"I've got that covered."

After waiting in line at Black's for twenty minutes, Kait and I were staring at the biggest beef rib we'd ever seen along with a half pound of wet (aka fatty) brisket and some sausage. Black's is known for their beef ribs, and we could see why. The rib was nicely marbled, and the meat fell right off the bone. Their BBQ sauce is tangy and went perfectly with the smoke flavor from the meat. The brisket and sausage was good, but didn't compare to the rib. Of course we saved some for Leo who was patiently waiting for us to return.

As expected, the grocery store was packed. We always try to find the local chains as we travel. Here in Texas, H-E-B is not only the local chain, but a popular destination for shoppers due to their endless samples. I tried different beers, a couple wines, an assortment of sausages and tamales. I didn't think I had any room left after BBQ, but apparently I was mistaken. H-E-B certainly beats any of the grocery stores we had back in California, and I can see why Texans love this place. A bulb of fresh garlic, a pound of imported parmesan and two heads of cauliflower later, I had what I needed for our side dish and we headed home.

Thanksgiving morning was like any other—a pot of Chemex coffee while we sat and relaxed. I no longer have to worry about leaving for work or thinking that Monday is only a day away. Every day is a weekend and we have the freedom to do whatever we like. It's rewarding to be the master of my own destiny now, rather than subject to the whims of a company. I can finally say I'm living the life that I want.

As content as I was sitting there drinking my coffee, I realized I was missing something. We wouldn't be driving over to my mom's house later today and I began to feel a bit homesick. Thanksgiving is always a big holiday celebration for my family. We started a tradition of inviting anyone and everyone to come over and would end up having twenty or more people show up. When I spoke to my mom yesterday, she was telling me who all was coming over and everything she was making, including three turkeys (one just for extra gravy!), and it's really making me miss being in Los Angeles.

After coffee we took Leo for a walk around the park. At the far corner of the park I began to see some of the devastation from the storm. There is a gully that runs alongside the park where we saw multiple trailers that had been swept away by the river. One was still hanging from a large tree, and the others were smashed on top of one another. We saw picnic tables, bikes and various other things hanging from trees. It was scary to think this tame river had done all that damage just a few months ago.

It reminded me of our second night at the RV park in Pagosa Springs, Colorado. Our site was next to a small river, and that evening, as rain began to pound the motorhome, we got a flash flood warning and flood advisory for the river we were camped ten feet from.

The campground was pitch black, and with the heavy rain, we didn't want to try driving through it to find another spot on higher ground. We were worried that we may not see a tree branch or electrical box and run into it. Instead, we devised a plan. I picked a spot along the bank that if the water reached that point, we'd leave. We brought the slides in, put everything away and got ready to bug out. Kait would drive the Jeep and I'd try to follow in the motorhome.

I spent most of the night checking the river. Fortunately, the river never flooded, but it did emphasize the fact that we needed to become much more aware of weather conditions. We got a better weather app, and since then we check it frequently and make sure we always know what the weather will be anywhere we are going.

Staring at the destruction the river had caused, Kait pulled out her phone, opened the weather app and said, "There is a storm watch and it's supposed to rain pretty hard tonight. Do you think we should be worried?"

"I don't know. Let's ask the staff when we go to the potluck later. This river has already flooded twice this year, and I don't want to be around for the third time. Come on, I need to get back so I can make our side dish."

Spaghetti and Cauliflower is a family recipe brought over from Italy by my father's side of the family. It's the one dish that he was always in charge of making in our house. Growing up, I'd always watch and get yelled at for trying to grab a piece of cauliflower while my father was mixing everything. Eventually I'd seen him do it enough and learned to make it myself. Anytime we serve spaghetti and cauliflower for people, they love it. It doesn't matter if they hate cauliflower, everyone loves it. For this occasion, I decided to skip the spaghetti and double the amount of cauliflower I used, turning it from a meal to a side dish. Voila!

Making this dish back in our old house, I had a large pot to boil all of the cauliflower and an even larger frying pan to sauté the cauliflower in the garlic and olive oil. However in our small kitchen, I can't fit our pot and fry pan on the stove at the same time, so I had to make everything in shifts and it took twice as long.

At the potluck, we really enjoyed ourselves and met some nice people. It was the first time I'd ever had smoked turkey and was in love with the Cajun version they had. Of course, it was from H-E-B. As far as the side dishes were concerned, the cauliflower was the first to go. People loved it and kept coming back for more until all that was left were a few small pieces of garlic. After a few trips to the dessert table, Kait and I had to roll ourselves out of there. I'm full just thinking about that meal!

Back at the motorhome, Kait asks, "Did you ask anyone about the rain tonight?"

"I did. They told me that they don't expect the storm to be bad enough to cause flooding. If anything does happen, they'll go door to door and warn people. What's the weather app say?"

"Radar images look pretty nasty," Kait says, holding her phone up. "It looks like the center of the storm is going to pass right over us. Maybe we should put the slides in just in case."

"I think we'll be fine. They didn't seem to be concerned."

11:30 that night I changed my mind. The wind was blowing so hard that our motorhome was rocking side to side, even with the jacks down. I had read online that slides can exaggerate the effect of the wind, so we brought our slides in and got ready for the knock on the door. Luckily for us, the knock never came and the next day we headed out to Salt Lick BBQ for some more brisket and ribs. With two BBQ spots and a giant Thanksgiving feast in between, we probably put on about twenty pounds each. I feel like I'm back in college, putting on the "Freshman 15." At least we have Leo to keep us somewhat active.

Thursday, December 3rd, 2015

We're quickly approaching the anniversary of our third month on the road, a quarter of the way through our year. Traffic to the website is starting to pick up and we made $19.37 in November from the website and the few videos we posted on YouTube. We shared a celebratory high-five because we hit our goal of covering the cost of the coffee I consume when working at different coffee shops.

On average, we're each putting in twenty hours a week worth of work. I made the mistake of calculating our hourly earnings which is depressing, but we are seeing growth and that is encouraging. That said, we're a far cry from putting a dent in the $2,800 or so we are spending each month. We still have nine months to make it work, but time is flying by. Regardless of how small a dent we were making, Kait and I are about to commit ourselves fully to this new lifestyle.

Before leaving California we researched changing our domicile state. Being domiciled in California makes us subject to some of the highest taxes, vehicle registration fees and insurance rates in the country. We're paying over $2,000 a year on the motorhome alone in registration fees and insurance. The trouble with changing your state of residence is that most states require that you have some type of permanent address, like an apartment or house. Florida, Texas and South Dakota, however, allow you to use an address from a mail service as your "permanent residence."

Neither Kait nor I have ever been to South Dakota, and we want to pick a state where we at least have some friends or family. This helped us narrow down to Florida and Texas. Both have very friendly attitudes towards full-time RVers and no state income tax. Initially, Florida was our first choice because residents get special discounts at Walt Disney World, on cruises and many other attractions in the state. The problem is that we want to change our state of residency before the new year, and since it's already December, we don't want to rush trying to get to Florida. So we decided to become Texans.

In Texas, to become a resident, we need to have an address. There is a company called Escapees that provides a mail service to RVers and will assign you an address when you become a member and sign up for their mail service. Texas recognizes this "mailbox" as a permanent address which will allow us to change our domicile state, get Texas driver's licenses, vehicle registration and lower rates on insurance compared to Los Angeles.

6:50 a.m.

It was freezing in the motorhome. We pulled into the Escapees RV park in Livingston last night. The only availability they had were a few dry camping spots and we're only allowed to run our generator at very specific hours, so we went all night without any heat since the generator is needed to run the heat pump. While we have a propane furnace, it's loud and we'd rather just throw an extra blanket on the bed. One trick we learned to conserve electricity is that when it's this cold, we turn the fridge off so it's not running all night. Considering it is in the mid-forties in the motorhome, we aren't worried about anything spoiling.

Normally, we never wake up this early, but we are excited because this will (hopefully) be our first day as Texans. I've spent thirty-five years as a Californian and leaving that state to become a Texan is a symbol to me that we have no plans to go back.

The Escapees office opened at eight and we walk through the doors shortly after. "Good morning," Kait says to the woman at the counter. "We're here to sign up for your mail forwarding service."

"Great, have a seat and someone will be up in a few minutes to help get everything set up for y'all."

"Thank you," Kait replies, then walks back to where I am sitting. "Honey, if we're going to be Texans we're going to have to start saying 'y'all.'"

I start laughing at the thought of Kait walking around saying "y'all" and a few minutes later, a friendly woman comes out to greet us. She shows us around the facility before getting our paperwork taken care of. After filling out and signing a few forms, we are given our membership card and new Texas address.

We went with the basic mail service Escapees offers. This gives us a permanent address in Livingston, and when mail is sent there, they hold it for us until we call to request it. They will then forward our mail to wherever we happen to be and deduct the cost from our postage balance. Add-ons include a service where Escapees will open and scan your mail so you can look at it online, but we figure the basic service will work just fine for us. Kait and I had discussed using a friend or family member's address for our mail, but we didn't want to burden them with having to send everything to us whenever we called.

After returning to the motorhome, my first call is to our insurance company to switch our address from California to

Texas. In order to get a driver's license, Texas requires two forms of proof of residency. Vehicle insurance is accepted as one of those. We'd been having trouble getting cell service but we got lucky this morning because the call dropped right as the customer service agent was thanking us for our business.

With our new policy in hand, we took the Jeep and motorhome to have them inspected. In Texas, vehicles have to be inspected each year in order to be registered. One of the reasons we chose Texas was because if your vehicle is out of state when it comes time to register, then you can forgo the inspection until the vehicle returns to the state. This will be handy so we don't have to plan to be back in the state each year around registration time. The inspections take less than thirty minutes, performed by a local mechanic. When we're ready to leave, there is a line of motorhomes waiting. Apparently it pays to be the first out of the Escapees office.

Just past noon with paperwork in hand, we head to the Polk County Tax Office. Coming from Los Angeles, we are both accustomed to going to the DMV and waiting for hours to get anything done. Here, we walk right up to the counter where a very nice woman greets us. The process for registering our vehicles takes about an hour because we had to take a few pictures of the motorhome and email them to the office so they could complete our application. When it came time to pay, we were amazed. It cost us 50% less to register all of our vehicles in Texas than one vehicle in California.

Now that we had our new vehicle registration documents which can be used as the second form of proof of residency, we headed down the street to the Texas Department of Public Safety for our new driver's licenses. We arrived at the office just after their lunch break, and only one person was working. However, as over worked as the woman behind the counter is, she is just a nice as everyone else we've met today and got us taken care of quickly. By 3:30 p.m. we were officially Texas residents.

Ironically, two days later, we left Texas and continued east into Louisiana.

BONUS CONTENT: More information about choosing a domicile state and how to become a Texan can be found here: https://weretherussos.com/how-to-become-texas-residents/

13. LOUISIANA

Saturday, December 5th, 2015

Have you ever eaten something and said, "This is delicious but I think I'm having a heart attack." Those were my exact words sitting in the parking lot of Billy's Boudin and Cracklin.

Bouncing along Interstate 10 (the highway here is so bad, you literally bounce) into Lafayette, Louisiana, Kait insisted we find a place for boudin. It's a local specialty she told me and it has been on her list of foods to try. Her research led us to Billy's which had good reviews and a parking lot that could accommodate our motorhome. When we want to pull off the interstate to check out a place, we have to plan in advance. That usually entails the person in the passenger seat calling the establishment and asking if they have parking for RVs and sometimes even disconnecting the Jeep before we arrive. I could tell Kait was relieved when the woman at Billy's told her the parking lot wasn't very full so we shouldn't have any problems finding a place to park.

The restaurant was right off the highway, and I stayed behind to take Leo for a bathroom break while Kait went inside. In the twenty minutes she was in there, cars, trucks and other motorhomes came and went. It was an endless cycle of people who would walk in and come out with a brown paper bag dotted with oil.

When Kait finally made it back to the motorhome, she had two bags in hand. In the time it took her to walk across the parking lot, the bags became translucent from all the oil that had soaked into them. "This is going to be good," I said to myself.

"Okay honey, I was only going to get us a few boudin balls to try but then I saw the cracklin so I bought some of each. Here is a pepper jack boudin ball to start. You should have seen all the stuff they had in there. It looked amazing."

As Kait tried handing me the boudin ball, Leo almost snatched it from her hand. He seemed as excited as I was, but Kait managed to pass me the greasy delicacy without Leo intercepting it.

"You'd better keep an eye on those bags," I said.

Biting into the boudin ball, I broke through the outer shell and into a moist sausage and pepper jack cheese filling. The flavors were overwhelming. As I savored the greasy goodness, Kait explained that the balls were made from boudin sausage and then deep fried. It was amazing but I felt my heart miss a beat as it struggled to process what I was putting in my body.

Reaching over, I put my hand into the bag of cracklin and pulled out what looked like a deep fried slab of bacon covered in seasoning. It was still warm when I bit into it and even more amazing than the boudin ball. "There's no way I could live here. I'd be eating this stuff all the time," I told Kait.

"Do you want me to go back in and get some more?"

"No, it's better you don't. Three of those balls and half that bag of cracklin is going to be more than enough."

After our indulgence, we headed to a nearby Cracker Barrel to spend the night. Driving up to the restaurant, we passed a gas station where a couple groups of ne'er-do-wells were standing around various cars. One group was yelling at another, and as we passed, the hairs on the back of my neck went up. I didn't know if a fight was about to break out or what, but something in my gut told me that we shouldn't spend the night in that area. When I mentioned it to Kait, she remarked that she had the same feeling and was worried about leaving the motorhome here if we ventured out, so we decided to try and find another place to spend the night.

Kait had found two Walmarts in the area that allowed overnight parking so we decided to park the motorhome at the Cracker Barrel and take the Jeep to go scout them. I was worried about leaving our motorhome, but at seven miles per gallon, it could get costly driving it all over town. We agreed that if the rest of Lafayette was like this, we'd get back on the road and go somewhere else.

When we arrived at the first Walmart, I almost told Kait we were heading back to the motorhome and leaving. I got that same feeling in my gut. More groups of guys just loitering in the parking lot and an absence of any other RVs, which is a rarity at a Walmart that allows overnight parking. Everything in me was saying, "Leave now." I didn't have much hope of finding a place we'd be comfortable, but Kait kept looking. "There's another Walmart close to a Whole Foods," she said, looking at her phone.

"If there's a Whole Foods, then we should be good. Let's go check it out."

The second Walmart was completely different. It was amazing, only a few miles from where we'd been, and the city had completely changed. There were a few other motorhomes parked in the lot with a couple big rigs, and I felt much better about staying there.

When I got up the next morning, I could tell Kait had been up for a few hours by the way she was studying her phone. Walking into the living room, she looked up at me with pleading eyes and said, "I've been researching Lafayette, and people say that it has some of the best food in Louisiana. There's this place I read about that's supposed to have an amazing brunch. I know we're watching our expenses, but I would really like to splurge and try some of the best food Louisiana has to offer."

I started laughing and said, "Do you really think I would complain if you want to go out to get some of the best food in Louisiana? I know we've been trying to save money but part of seeing the country is getting to experience the food. I think we can go out to eat every now and again when we find something we really want."

"Really?" Kait asked in an excited voice, and before I had a chance to respond she said, "Because there's this place I want to try that has amazing po'boys and I want to go see the Tabasco factory."

"Anything you want, my love," I said with a laugh, as I got out of bed to go start some coffee.

While I enjoyed my coffee and relaxed, Kait sat down to work on our website. She loves working in the mornings while I prefer to work in the evening. Typically she'll work from the couch so she can spread out with Leo passed out at her feet. I like to work from the passenger seat. There is a small folding desk that pulls out from the wall that is just big enough for my laptop and mouse.

Our first stop was a well-known restaurant for brunch. When we sat down, Kait explained to our waitress that she'd read all about this place and asked what were some of her favorite things. The waitress's eyes lit up, and she gave us a list of things we had to try. First up was an order of beignets. Light, fluffy and sprinkled with a generous amount of powdered sugar, these little balls of heaven were the best we've ever had (and, yes, we've been to Cafe Du Monde) and went perfectly with my cup of chicory coffee. Kait ordered the gumbo, which was out of this world. After a few bites, Kait looked up and asked, "How did they infuse all of this flavor into the roux?" My fried chicken and waffles were so delicious that I considered asking for a steak knife in order to defend against attacks from Kait trying to steal a piece.

With full bellies, we took a drive to Avery Island to tour the Tabasco factory. It's $1 to get across the bridge and onto the privately-owned island to reach the factory. Unfortunately the factory was closed for tours while we were there, but they made up for it with enough samples in their gift shop to make even the most hungry person walk away full. They had every type of Tabasco there...along with even more I never knew existed, including Tabasco ice cream and a special reserve Tabasco made from distilled white vinegar. After trying almost every type, we picked up bottles of our favorites, Garlic and Chipotle, then headed back into town.

We spent the rest of the day working at a coffee shop until hunger struck again. It was time to head to Old Thyme Grocery. The local favorite is their fried shrimp po'boy. Neither of us felt like we could eat a whole sandwich, so we decided to share one and grabbed a table outside so Leo could join us. The sandwich was simple. A soft roll stuffed with lightly battered shrimp, slightly wilted lettuce, tomato and some mayo. I shook some Crystal hot sauce on my half and went to town. I was in heaven after that first bite. The shrimp were plump, sweet, lightly fried and went perfectly with the mayo and Crystal. That sandwich was one of the best I've ever had.

As much as we are enjoying the food in Lafayette, we have to get back on the road and head to New Orleans to meet a friend. He is flying out to join us, and we want to get there a few days early so we can get settled before his arrival.

Monday, December 7th, 2015

"This is the worst road I've ever been on," I said to Kait from the driver's seat of the motorhome shortly after we left Lafayette. Each expansion joint on Interstate 10 was like going over a ledge and would produce a jaw-jarring thump. It was so bad I was worried that the cabinets above the driver's area would fall on top of us. To combat the punishment, I slowed to about fifty miles an hour. As the larger trucks flew past me, it sounded like their loads were going to bounce right off the trailer. This stretch lasted for thirty miles before we got any kind of reprieve, but luckily we made it through with no issues.

"Let's never take this route again," Kait said as I started driving across the Aftachalaya Basin.

"Absolutely. Is there another way around?"

"There is, but it would take twice as long."

"I'm fine with that if we don't have to drive across that again. Let's just not forget if we ever have to drive back this way," I said. "I wonder what that would have been like in a diesel pusher?"

I asked this question because our gas motorhome is built on the Ford F53 chassis with the V10 gas engine. One of the biggest complaints about the Ford chassis is that the ride is poor compared to diesels. People spend thousands of dollars to try to get it to be more comfortable. When Kait and I were shopping for a motorhome, we considered buying a diesel motorhome which have air-ride suspension. While we haven't been bothered by our motorhome's ride until now, I wonder if the extra $80-100k would have done much to help with the ride today.

Since we weren't quite sure when we would arrive in New Orleans, or leave for that matter, we didn't make any campground reservations. There is a campground right in the center of the city, but it's way beyond our budget, so on our drive down, Kait started calling around. She found a state park with a campground called Bayou Segnette State Park just outside of New Orleans. Although it would be a bit of a drive into the city, after spending so much time camping on public land, we'd rather have some peace and quiet and make the drive in when we want to explore.

The last time we were in New Orleans, I was in town for a work conference, and Kait decided to join me. While I was in and out of meetings and seminars, she was out exploring the city. At the end of each day I would meet her at a local restaurant where we savored the local cuisine, and she would give me a full recount of all the amazing food she devoured without me. "Let's plan a vacation so we can go back to some of these places and really enjoy them," she would say.

Needless to say, I was eager to return to NOLA and try some of the delicious dishes I had heard so much about. We paid for a week at the campground and I know, one week isn't much time in a city that has so much to offer, but we figure we'll try our best to experience as much as possible.

Like any good trip to New Orleans, ours started with a walk around town to see the sights and build up a thirst in preparation for happy hour. Given how hot and humid it is, Leo decided that he would prefer to stay in the air conditioning, rather than venture into the city with us, so we were on our own.

Happy hour is something this town takes seriously. Virtually all establishments have some type of happy hour, and we decided to try a few out. Our first stop was Basin Seafood to share a local beer and a couple appetizers while I regaled Kait with tales of my first trip to New Orleans during a college spring break trip. Once she was satisfied that it was better she didn't know me in my early twenties, we strolled down to Superior Seafood. After ordering a dozen fifty-cent oysters and a two-for-one French 75 (alcoholic slushy drink), we began to pick the bartender's brain.

In touristy areas, it always helps to ask a local where the good spots are, and we did just that with the bartender. After chatting her up, we got the bill and then asked for a recommendation for dinner. She suggested a place for muffalettas that are to die for and then asked if we wanted a to-go cup.

"A to-go cup?" I asked with astonishment.

"Yeah so you can take the rest of your French 75 with you," she responded with a smile, holding up a styrofoam cup.

The 75s were a bit stronger than I expected, so I hadn't planned on finishing it, but I wanted to see where this was going, so asked, "Can I drink it while walking down the street?"

"Of course, as long as it isn't in a glass container."

"Wow. Anything else we should know?"

"Hm, well, you can drive with them too."

Now my curiosity was piqued. "It's legal to drink and drive here?"

"No, but as long as you have a lid on your drink and a piece of scotch tape over the hole for the straw, it's legal to drive with it. If you take the tape off, then it's considered an open container."

"Amazing," I said shaking my head. I thanked our bartender for the offer but declined the cup. Then Kait, our designated driver, drove us to Parran's for a fried seafood muffaletta. They're so large we had to share one...well, that, and we'd just spent the evening eating appetizers and oysters.

The next morning we were up early and off to the National WWII museum. One of the first displays visitors see when they enter is a Higgins Boat - the landing craft our US forces used for beach landings such as D-Day. Designed and built right here in New Orleans by Andrew Higgins, the Higgins boat was so crucial for our victory in the war that Eisenhower said, "He [Higgins] won the war for us." This is why the National WWII Museum is here in New Orleans.

The experience at the museum was awesome and emotional. I loved seeing all of the tanks, planes and various weapons of war. At the same time, I read the stories of those who fought with them and the hell they went through. I learned not only about what was going on overseas but also here at home. Unfortunately our time at the museum was limited because Leo was waiting for us back at the motorhome. When we left, Kait and I both agreed that we need to come back and spend a full day or two and be able to take in the full experience.

Friday, December 11th, 2015

One of our biggest concerns when we left our jobs was what we would do about health care. We decided that we would ride out the rest of 2015 with no coverage and then figure out what we wanted to do. With open enrollment almost over, we sat down to decide what to do.

The ACA (aka Obamacare) was really starting to ramp up but as we did our research, it didn't seem like the right choice for us. Instead, we opted for a plan through Costco. At $485 per month, it would allow us to see any doctor in network nationwide. Neither of us go to the doctor regularly, but we both wanted to be covered just in case and avoid the tax penalties for not having medical insurance.

With that out of the way, we decided it was time for lunch, so we headed to a cornerstone of New Orleans cuisine: the Commander's Palace. The temperature and the humidity subsided enough that we could bring Leo along and have him hang in the car while we had lunch. We've learned that on a cool day with the windows down, the Jeep stays about the same temperature as it is outside and, after a long walk, Leo is very content to sleep in the Jeep while we're off doing something.

"Honey, what are you going to have?" Kait asked as I'm studying the menu.

"I'm getting the three martini lunch."

"I didn't see that on the menu," Kait said looking at me with skepticism.

"Yeah, you get up to three for twenty-five cents each with any entree. It's right there on the menu," I say, pointing to the tiny text and reading, "Limit three per person 'cause that's enough.'"

"I'm going to order one too. For twenty-five cents I won't feel bad if I can't finish it!"

Lunch was fantastic. However, we didn't even manage to finish even one person's limit of martinis. Our friend John was arriving in a few hours, so we decided to leave the Jeep where it was and take Leo on a walking tour of the area to kill some time.

I met John a few years ago through an online motorcycle group I belonged to. We used to have meet-ups in different areas of Los Angeles, grab a bite to eat or something and then go for a ride. John and I both rode the same motorcycle, so we traded numbers and would meet on the weekends for a long ride or take our bikes up to the track and race. Motorcycles brought us together, and we've stayed good friends ever since.

Prior to leaving on this trip, we invited most of our friends to meet up with us on the road. They all seemed excited and told us they couldn't wait to join us someplace. However, three months in and John is the first person to join us on the road. I'm excited because, although I have Kait, I miss my friends. I had quite a few friends at work, and now that I don't see them, they're quickly fading from my life. I'm also tired of always having to go through the whole getting to know you routine with everyone we're meeting on the road. I'm really looking forward to being able to hang out with an old friend who already knows me and our story.

We met John at his hotel and headed towards Bourbon Street since it's his first time in the city. We brought Leo with us and decided to continue walking through the city and hit up all the touristy things. While the establishments aren't dog friendly, we took advantage of the to-go cups the waitress told us about and walked through the French Quarter with our adult beverages in hand. Strolling down Bourbon Street with Leo is definitely a different experience. Everyone wanted to pet Leo, especially the inebriated, and Kait had to keep an eye on some of them to make sure they didn't spill their brightly colored cocktails on his white fur.

The most fun we had with John was the jazz brunch at the Court of Two Sisters. Endless food, drinks and live jazz all set outside in a lovely courtyard area. The experience embodied so many things we love about New Orleans...the food, music and atmosphere. Something we'll definitely do again when we go back to the Big Easy.

As John was leaving to fly home, he said, "Trying to meetup with you two is like trying to land on an aircraft carrier. You have to find and hit this little spot out in the middle of the ocean, but when you do it's amazing. Thank you, both. I had a great time, and we'll have to do this again."

I was sad to see him leave. I enjoyed this time more than I had expected and it reminded me of the fun Kait and I had in our previous lives. Whenever I've talked about our lives before we hit the road, it was always about what we didn't like - our jobs, the city, etc. I hadn't stopped to think about how many things we loved about our old lives, especially being able to spend time with friends and family.

BONUS CONTENT: The National WWII Museum has become one of our favorite museums in the country. We highly recommend making a trip to NOLA to visit it. If you'd like more information, check out the article we put together about our time there (there's also a link at the end to an article about the campground we stayed at): https://weretherussos.com/the-national-wwii-museum/. Also, here is a round-up of our things to do in Nola article: https://weretherussos.com/things-to-do-in-new-orleans/

14. OUR FIRST VLOG

Monday, December 14th, 2015

"Ready to hit the road?" I asked.

"Are we all dumped and everything put away outside?"

"We're all set and I checked the tire pressures. Everything looks good."

"Okay. Florida, here we come," Kait said as she jumped into the driver's seat.

Since we'd made it this far east, we decided to push on to Florida for Christmas. My sister and brother-in-law are flying in for the holiday and are going to stay at his parents' farm in Central Florida. Since we missed spending time with family on Thanksgiving, we decided to make it to Florida so we could be with my sister and her husband's family. Once I told my sister we'd meet them there, she was over the moon with excitement.

When we were RV shopping last year, we flew out to stay with my brother-in-law's parents, Rick and Suzanne. They told us that once we had our motorhome, we were welcome to camp on their farm and use their place as a base for exploring the state. We said we'd be back and it's exciting to think that we'll be making good on our promise.

Although we could have made the drive in a day, we decided to take our time. Kait looked up a few cities along our route and found some fun things for us to do in Gainesville, Florida. With over a million snowbirds making their way south in RVs for the winter, and many of them headed to

Florida, we decided to make a campground reservation in advance and give ourselves some time to get there.

"Where do you want to stop tonight?" Kait asked once we're back on Interstate 10.

"We don't check in until Thursday, so we have three nights to kill. I wouldn't mind stopping in Panama City. I've always heard so much about that place, so I'd like to see it for myself."

"What have you heard?"

"You know, stories about spring break and it's been mentioned in different songs. I've just heard so much I feel like I have to see it."

"Okay, well Mobile, Alabama, is on the way and there is a 'friendly' Walmart. We can stop there tonight and then head to Panama City," Kait says, using our new nickname for Walmarts that allow overnight parking.

Tuesday, December 15th, 2015

Mobile was a bit of a bust. By the time we parked at Walmart and drove into the city, it was late and we were tired. Neither of us felt like getting out to walk around, so we headed back to Walmart to do some shopping. We grabbed a few different food items and then went to check out. Once we were rung up, Kait looked in shock at the cashier. Mobile has a ten-percent sales tax that applies to food items so Kait decided to put everything back. Her reasoning was that we could pick all of this stuff up tomorrow in Florida and not have to pay any tax. Another lesson learned, check local sales tax rates before you buy anything. Instead, we rented a movie from Redbox and relaxed in the motorhome. I promised to make my famous stove top popcorn to enjoy while we watched the movie from bed.

When we got on the road this morning for Panama City, I saw that a vlogger I follow who also RVs is in the city. We've enjoyed meeting like-minded people, so I sent him a message asking if he would like to meetup. Shortly after sending it, he wrote back that he would and we made plans to hang out that evening.

"So this is Panama City," I said as we drove down the main drag.

"You don't sound very impressed," Kait replied.

"I just expected more. I've heard these crazy stories about spring break but it just looks like a small, quiet town."

"Did you expect that the beach would be packed full of people partying?" Kait said with a laugh.

"Now that you mention it, that would be strange to see in mid-December."

The local Walmart became our home for the night once again as we pulled into the parking lot and found a spot as far from the store as possible. It's always a game trying to find the best place to park when we're spending the night at a Walmart. Park too far to the edge of the lot and you may have delivery trucks driving past all night. Park towards the middle and, at a twenty-four-hour location, you'll have people pushing shopping carts and cars driving by at all hours. Too close to other RVs and you may end up with a neighbor who's running their generator all night.

After an early dinner, we loaded Leo into the Jeep and headed over to meet the vlogger. He's camped about ten minutes from the Walmart and is spending the year traveling around the lower forty-eight with his wife. They're currently making their way west as we are going east, and it's just coincidence that we happened to end up in the same city at the same time.

When we arrive I feel like I already know him. I've been following his channel on YouTube since before we hit the road, and it's surreal to see him in person. We come to find out that he's also been following our blog but wants to know why we don't produce more video content. I tell him about our first experience trying to film something on our last day of work and what a disaster that was. I kind of froze up when Kait pointed the camera at me and really had nothing to say. We told him that while we thought making videos would be a great idea, neither of us wanted to be in front of the camera.

He was able to relate to the way we felt but told us that we just needed to do it and make our first vlog. Once we had that done, the next one would be easier and so on. It is just a matter of practicing and getting better at it until we're both as comfortable in front of the camera as we were sitting there talking to him. I could see his point but was still skeptical. What would we talk about, and who in their right mind would want to watch us?

We had a great evening, and as we were getting ready to go, he said, "Before you guys leave, I am going to put you in my vlog."

"Wait, what?" Kait asked nervously.

He tells us that he wants to introduce us to his audience and that he'll be publishing the vlog in a couple weeks. Until then we need to put up a couple vlogs so the people who come find us have something to watch. Kait and I both hesitate for a moment while we ponder his offer.

"Let's do it," I said to Kait.

The three of us stand up, and our new friend pushes the record button on his camera, holding it out using a selfie stick. The next few minutes go by in a flash, and I have no idea if half of what we said made any sense. It feels very strange to have a camera pointed at you and speak to a faceless crowd. It definitely helped that we had someone experienced there to hold our hand through the process. As we were walking out of the motorhome, he gave us the selfie stick and wished us luck.

On the ten-minute drive back, Kait and I brainstormed as to what kind of videos we want to make. As we were chatting, we fall back into the "Who would want to watch this?" mindset. Determined, I tell Kait that I'm going to suck it up and film something just to say I did and when we get back to the motorhome, I dig out our camera and tripod.

"Are you really going to film a vlog tonight?" Kait asked.

"I'm going to try."

I cleared off the table, set up the tripod and camera, pressed record and sat down across from it. For a long minute I just stared at the camera. My mind was blank. Reaching back across the table I stopped the camera and walked into the bedroom.

"I have nothing to say," I told Kait, who was laying in bed.

"Maybe talk about our day, the drive in and what that was like?"

Starting the camera back up, I sat down and said, "We drove into Panama City today and had an interesting drive.

As we were getting close to town a semi-truck cut us off, and when he did, it kicked up a large stone that put a chip in the motorhome's windshield. This is the third chip we've gotten and we're going to have to call the glass repair company again. I'm worried that one of these chips is going to turn into a larger crack."

I continued to talk but felt like I was rambling about nothing. Why would anyone be interested in watching me talking about our day while sitting at a table? After I finished, I walked back into the bedroom to see what Kait thought.

"I don't think it was very interesting," she said. "It just sounded like a stream of consciousness. Why don't we film our day-to-day adventures rather than just sitting in front of a camera. I think people would rather see the places we're going than listen to you talk about it."

"I get it. So rather than talk about the drive, actually film it."

"Exactly," Kait said before wishing me a good night.

"Time to wake up," Kait said, nudging me. "I want to go check out the beach before we leave this morning."

I could barely open my eyes. I only got a couple hours of sleep last night because I couldn't turn my brain off. Ideas were flying through my mind thinking about what our first vlog would be.

"I had an idea last night," I told Kait, rubbing my eyes and standing up. "I think we should film our time at the beach, walking around Panama City and generally talking about what we're doing." She agreed and put me in charge of getting everything set up.

Climbing in behind the wheel of the Jeep, I handed Kait the selfie stick with our GoPro mounted to it. "Just hold it out and kind of angle it toward me."

"What do you want to talk about?" Kait asked.

"Anything. Just whatever we'd normally talk about."

"Okay, you start."

Nothing. I was drawing a blank again and began to have flashbacks of the first video we tried to shoot and what a disaster that was.

"Don't think about it," Kait said, seeing the frustration on my face. "Just start talking. We can edit it later, but you have to start somewhere. The more you do it, the better you'll get."

I closed my eyes taking a long, deep breath. When I opened my eyes, I put the Jeep in drive, looked at the camera and said, "Good morning. Um. What day is it? Today is December 16th and it's day number ninety-five of our trip. Um. Please excuse me because I haven't had my coffee yet..." I continued to talk on our drive and began to get a bit more comfortable.

Our time at the beach with the camera was a bit strange. We really didn't know what to say to each other, and I felt like all of our attention was spent focusing on the act of filming and rather than the actual experience of being on the beach in Panama City. I'm sure it will become easier as we go, but right now, I can't see us living life through a lens.

After leaving the beach, we headed back to the motorhome and got on the road. We're heading to Tallahassee today because we're getting low on food, and there's a Costco next to a Walmart that allows overnight parking. I swear, with the amount of time we're spending at Walmarts, it could be considered our new home.

"I can't believe this rain," I tell Kait as we're driving along State Road 20.

"Hold on, save it for the camera," she said, grabbing the GoPro. "Okay, you were saying?"

"I can't believe this rain. There are trucks pulled along the side of the road and it's really coming down hard," I say to the camera.

Kait stopped the recording and said, "Honey, when you have something to say, say it on camera. You have to remember to always be filming if you want to vlog."

"I know, it's just not something I think about."

It was still raining when we pulled into the Costco parking lot. I got in line at the gas station and patiently waited for the two cars ahead of me to finish. I look down to reset the trip odometer and check our total miles. "We're almost at 8,000 miles," I said to Kait as she was getting ready to take Leo out for a potty break. "I'm going to head over to Walmart tonight and buy oil and an oil filter for the motorhome."

"Where are you going to change it?"

"At Rick and Suzanne's place when we get down there."

Our Costco shopping trip goes well, but Kait reminds me I should have brought the camera with us to film while we were going through the store. The most difficult thing about vlogging is going to be remembering to not only bring a camera but to hit the record button.

Walking back to the motorhome, I tell Kait to wait outside while I run in and grab the GoPro. Coming back out, I started recording. "Okay, tell everyone what we got," I said.

Kait showed off our shopping cart full of food. The last Costco we went to was in Tucson and we're hoping this haul lasts at least a month, so the cart is completely full. As Kait's going through the cart, she makes sure to point out the wine.

"We had to pick up some wine because we're going to be visiting family and we all like to sit and have a glass of wine at lunch, mid-lunch, mid-afternoon break, dinner and post dinner so we stocked up on some wine."

Kait is getting the hang of this. She has a great personality, is funny and really engaging with the camera. I still have a lot to iron out, but if I don't get much better, Kait can be our on-camera personality. She's got the pretty face for it anyway.

After we get the food all stored away in the motorhome, we drive over to Walmart and find our parking spot for the night.

"I'm heading into the store. Do you want to go?" I asked.

"No, I'm tired. Have fun; just don't go crazy buying stuff."

"Alright," I said with a laugh and headed out. As I got about ten feet from the motorhome, I realized I forgot something.

"Is this what you came back for?" Kait asked as she opened the door, holding out the GoPro.

"How'd you know?" I asked with a wink.

The idea was to film myself walking around Walmart, but I started feeling very self-conscious. I didn't want to be "that person" walking around the store holding a camera in front of their face.

When I reached the automotive section, it was empty, so I decided to make a quick video and then grab everything I needed. Holding down the power button, there was a very audible "beep beep beep" as the camera powered on. I looked around but no one seemed to have noticed. I pressed record, held the camera up and began speaking in a soft voice, "I'm currently at Walmart, in the automotive section and..."

"Excuse me sir, do you need help?" A Walmart employee asked, looking around the corner of a display he's stocking. I must have missed him.

"Uh, no, I'm fine. Thank you."

That didn't work. I walked to the other end of the automotive section, and started the camera again and right before I began to speak, an older man walked down the aisle and began looking for something. People were everywhere in the store, and I began to feel like I would never get the shot.

I walked to another area and spotted the employee again. He looked at me, wondering why I've returned. I probably looked like I was trying to steal something rather than get a quick video clip of me shopping.

I gave up and went to find the oil and filter and pick up a couple bottles of differential fluid for the Jeep. With all the towing, I want to make sure the fluid in there is fresh. I began walking back towards the front of the store and decide to just shoot the video and not worry about what other people think. I describe what I've picked up and I got a couple strange looks, but I didn't care. This would never work if I couldn't talk to a camera in front of other people.

"How'd it go?" Kait asked when I walked back into the motorhome. "You were gone for a while."

"Well, it was hard. I was getting stage fright trying to film in front of other people, but eventually I just said screw it and shot the video. I also went into Bass Pro Shops and grabbed a few shots."

"That's great. I'm proud of you. When do you think you'll edit the video?"

"I was planning on doing it tonight and then uploading it to YouTube. I thought it would be cool to try and upload videos the day we film them so it's timely."

"Great idea. Just let me know when you're done. I'd like to watch it before you make it public."

In college, I got my degree in computer graphics. My plan was to get into the video game industry but that never panned out. I figured I'd never use what I learned in school, but I'm realizing now that it's going to come in pretty handy.

It's been about thirteen years, but as I sat down at my computer and started playing with the video editing software, it all came back. Each video clip had to first be transferred from the GoPro's memory card onto my computer. After everything was on my computer, I started a project in iMovie and then added the first video file in the timeline, watched it, cut it and then added the second clip, marrying it to the first and editing out anything that's not interesting. I became lost in the computer until the final clip of me walking back to the motorhome with all my goodies from Walmart is in the video.

Standing up and stretching, I went into the bedroom with my laptop and sat it on the bed. Kait looked up from her phone and asked, "Are you finished already?"

"Yep," I said proudly. "Ready for you to take a look at it."

"Ohh, I'm so excited!" Kait took my laptop and pressed play. When the video ended, she stared at the screen for a moment and then looked up. "I really like it, but it feels long in certain parts like when we're at the beach. Can we go through it together and make changes?"

As we went through the video and she pointed out each change, I saw her vision. Cut out a little dialogue here, trim the end of a clip there and so on. By the time we were done, the video was much more interesting and flowed better.

"Thank you for your help. I think the video came out really well," I told Kait.

"Are you going to upload it?" She asked.

"Yes, right now. Do you think we have enough data for me to use my phone as a hot spot?"

"We should be fine and the video file isn't that big."

At 8:48 p.m., our first vlog had been uploaded to YouTube. I felt like this was the first step towards something new, and was excited to film the next one. I'll admit, it was frustrating at times and it will take a few more to really get comfortable, but I thought the final product was great. It was fun for me to sit down, edit the video and watch Kait and I go through our day. As long as it's fun, I can see us doing many more of these. I just hope people watching the video find it interesting.

Over the course of the next couple weeks, we filmed a few more vlogs about our travels to the farm and a how-to video on changing the oil in our motorhome. After that, we decided to take some time off to enjoy time with family. Kait shared the videos on our website and Facebook page, so we were getting a handful of views but nothing to write home about. I learned that it takes most vloggers months, if not a year or more to really establish an audience. We didn't want to give up, so on New Year's day, we made a commitment to make video production part of our strategy to grow our business into something that will sustain us.

BONUS CONTENT: Of course I have to share a link to that first vlog of ours: https://youtu.be/o7Ws9OCTER4 It's fun to go back and watch to see how far we've come since then. Also, here is the video we shot on our last day of work, which we thought was a disaster and said we'd never do it again: https://youtu.be/i7DU46czw00

15. TAMPA RV SHOW

Tuesday, January 12th, 2016

"I can't believe we've been in Florida for almost a month," I said to Kait.

"I know," Kait replied. "But here we are."

"There's still a lot of the state to see and I'd love to see the coasts and southern Florida."

"Well," Kait said, looking at the map on her phone, "we can head south along the Gulf Coast once we're done at the show."

The Florida RV SuperShow is one of the largest RV shows in the country, and we're here to make some videos. Although we don't have a solid plan, we'd like to make videos about the show highlighting the various RVs we find along the way. The show doesn't officially start until tomorrow, but we have media passes to get into Industry Day, which started earlier in the day. Kait was able to get the media passes since we'll be covering the show for our website and YouTube channel.

After we posted our first vlog about our time in Panama City, we've continued making videos for our YouTube channel. After New Years, we published a series of videos about our trip to Walt Disney World (First video: https://youtu.be/FjHWL28GquA). We haven't gotten many views on the videos yet, but the introduction video our new vlogger friend made was just posted. Our subscriber count has been going up steadily and, last I checked, we were in the 70s.

"Do you know where we're supposed to go?" Kait asked as we approached the fairgrounds.

"No clue. Let's park the motorhome in that open lot and drive the Jeep around to see if we can find where our campsite is."

"I hope we don't have to park over there," Kait said, pointing to a large field with massive generators.

"We're in the vendor camping area. Let's find the show office, get our media passes and find out where we're camping."

The fairgrounds are a beehive of activity. The show office is organized chaos but we manage to find our contact. She gives us a packet of information, badges and then calls someone on the radio to show us where our campsite is before taking off to put out another fire.

Walking out of the office, we're met by an employee who has us follow him in his golf cart to the camping area. The sites are nearly full with vendors who've been here for almost a week getting their booths set up. He leads us to a nice open grass area where they have electric hookups and sewer dumps. Once we stop, he informs us that the big generators we saw in the main field are to supply the electric hookups for all the people expected to camp on-site. "Tonight those fields will be almost full and the generators will be running 24/7," he tells us.

There aren't assigned spots, so we grab an end spot that's still open and back the motorhome in.

"I say we get set up, plug in, and then we can go walk around the show," Kait suggested.

"Good idea, we can put the AC on for Leo. I'll get us hooked up if you want to grab our camera gear."

"I wonder if people are going to take us seriously as media walking around with a GoPro?" Kait asked.

"Good point," I said with a chuckle. "We're going to be those amateurs walking around. If things on the channel pick up, maybe we can buy something a little more professional looking."

With the AC set to sixty-five, Leo gives us a brief look as we're walking out the door then jumps on the couch. We never expected it to be this hot in Florida in the middle of January, but it's been getting into the mid to high eighties with close to one-hundred percent humidity. When we lived in Los Angeles and it would get into the nineties and hundreds, Leo would go outside and sun bathe. In the Florida humidity, he prefers the AC. Can't say I blame him and I'm actually jealous he gets to relax in the cool air while we're walking around outside.

The last RV show we went to was over a year ago when we were still shopping for a motorhome. At the time it was completely overwhelming. We had no idea what we wanted and were lured in by all of the high-dollar rigs. We left that show with more questions than answers and haven't been to another RV show since. We're curious to see what we think now that we've been on the road for five months. More than anything, I'm exited to shoot some video. We've been working hard on improving our videos by tightening up our editing and trying to have an idea of what we want to shoot before we start. I've also become much more comfortable in front of the camera, especially in public.

Walking through the rear entrance, we flash our media badges and are completely overwhelmed by the size of the show. Since it's Industry Day, the show is not open to the public and it's not crowded. It looks like some vendors are still setting up while others are walking the show, checking out the competition.

"Where should we start?" I asked.

"Let's take a walk around and get a lay of the land. Then we can figure out what we want to shoot."

The first RV show we went to was big, but this is on another scale. As we walk, we see every type of RV there is. The show is a contrast from small teardrop trailers with few amenities to million dollar rigs that are nicer than most people's homes. Surprisingly, the small trailers seem to be drawing more of a crowd. The show is mostly outdoors, but there are a couple large, slightly air conditioned buildings with more RV dealers and vendors selling everything from RV accessories to beef jerky and jewelry.

After a few hours of walking around the show, my shirt is soaked with sweat, and we both need something to eat, so we head back to the motorhome to take a break. Opening the door to the motorhome, we feel a blast of cool air. "Oh that feels good!" I say to Leo who barely looks up to acknowledge our return and quickly goes back to sleep.

After lunch, we all take a short nap and relax. The heat of the afternoon seems to be tapering off a bit, so we head back to the show with Leo so he can get a good walk in. It's cooled down considerably and Leo seems excited.

I get shots of us as we're walking through the show and suggest that we check out the vendor halls. I figure it will be a good day to film before everything is open to the public. Kait is open to the idea and I also suggest that we film a couple walk-through videos of different RVs. They seem popular and simple enough. Walk-through the RV pointing out different features and showing people what it's like inside and out.

"Leo, it's okay," I say as I open the door to the first vendor hall. "There's carpet and it's air conditioned."

As Leo has become older, he's become skittish of buildings he's not familiar with. That mixed with his fear of slippery floors means it's sometimes difficult, if not impossible, to get him inside certain places. He's poking his head into the door I have propped open for him and checking to see if what I'm promising is true. Whether it's the cool air coming from inside or the carpet waiting just past the entry, Leo decides he's good with this place and walks tentatively inside as I press the record button on our GoPro. Each row we walk down reveals that most vendors have already left for the day. Since there isn't much to film, we decide to return tomorrow and spend the remainder of our day shooting RV walk-throughs.

Leaving the hall, my eyes go wide. "Now THAT is a motorhome!" I exclaim to Kait who is now pointing the camera at me. "If you don't mind holding Leo, I'm going to go in and check this thing out," I tell her.

"Don't forget the camera," Kait says with a smile, holding the GoPro out to me.

Grabbing the camera, I turn and race toward the massive motorhome in front of me. It looks like a giant Class C motorhome about forty-five feet long, built on a full-size

Freightliner semi-truck chassis. Stepping inside, I'm struck by how tall the ceilings are and can't stop looking up.

"The ceiling height is seven foot, eight," the salesman says with a smile.

"That's pretty incredible," I say. "I haven't seen many motorhomes with a ceiling that high."

"That's one of the things that makes ShowHauler stand out," he replies.

"What model is this?" I ask.

"All of our units are custom built, so we don't really have models. You can pick any length and layout you want. We also let you choose the chassis that you want to build on, assuming it meets our requirements."

"Do you mind if I go through the motorhome and shoot some video?" I ask holding up the GoPro.

"Not at all. If you have any questions, just let me know."

Hitting record on the GoPro, I start in the bedroom, opening cabinets and talking about everything I see. The GoPro is mounted on a small tripod that I'm using as a selfie stick. I have no idea what the video is going to look like because our GoPro doesn't have a screen, but it does have a wide angle lens which should be getting (almost) everything in frame.

The walk-through only takes me about five minutes to complete. I'm impressed with the quality of the motorhome but also surprised that it's under half a million dollars. Considering it's custom built, I thought it would be almost double that.

"What did you think?" Kait asks as I walk down the steps.

"It's really nice. You should go in and take a look. This is what I would want to get if we could afford it. It's all custom made with solid wood cabinets and doors."

"Not today," Kait says. "I want to go take a look at that van." She's pointing to a red Mercedes Sprinter van that appears to be 4x4 with a pop-top.

"I've heard of Sportsmobile," I tell Kait. "Let's go see if they'll let us do a walk-through of that."

The crew at Sportsmobile are excited to show off the van and give us a full tour, allowing us to film it. It's a cool rig and something I could see us taking out for the weekend but not much longer. It doesn't have a bathroom, only a porta-potty that you have to pull out of a cabinet to use. The van's roof isn't high enough to stand in unless you have the pop-top up. Regardless, the van looks like it could go anywhere, and it has piqued our interest.

After we get done filming the Sportsmobile, Kait sees a Winnebago View that she wants to check out. It's a smaller Class C motorhome built on the Mercedes Sprinter chassis. Since she is the one interested in the View, I film her doing the walk-through.

After Kait is done going through the motorhome, she tells me she could live in something that size. I don't see how, with the three of us and all of the stuff we have, there would never be enough room. Kait reminds me that we don't use half the stuff we brought and haven't touched most of what's stored in the bays. She makes me promise that when the show is over, we can go through the motorhome and do some spring cleaning.

"Regardless of how much stuff we get rid of, I still think it would be too small," I tell her. "What I really liked was that ShowHauler, but I'm happy with our Newmar."

"I am too, but having something this small would allow us to not worry about parking or driving such a large motorhome."

It's dark by the time we make it back to our motorhome, and we're wiped out from the heat and all the walking. As much as I would like to take the rest of the night off, I decided to get the video edited and live as soon as possible. We both agree with content like this that's timely, it's best to get it up quickly so people searching for the RV show can find it.

"Do you think we should brand the motorhome?" Kait asks as I am downloading the files from the GoPro. "When we were walking around earlier, I noticed most of the vendor RVs have their logos and websites on them."

"What are you thinking? Get our logo printed as a decal and put it up somewhere?"

"Yeah, I think it would be a good way to promote We're the Russos."

"Great idea. Once I'm done with the video, I'll work on putting something together that we can get printed."

Most of our vlogs have been pretty straightforward. We record a portion of our day; then I piece it together. It's quick and easy because everything is in sequential order, but the video we shot today is taking a lot more time. My goal is to try and tell a story about our time at the show, which has turned out to be much more difficult than I thought. Instead of laying out all the video footage in the order we filmed it, I work in shots of us walking through the show as transitions between the different walk-throughs. By midnight I've got a rough cut done for Kait to watch and a version of our logo I think would look good on the motorhome, except she's already sound asleep.

"I love the video," Kait says over coffee the next morning. "I have a few changes for you but once those are made, we can get it uploaded."

"What do you think about the decal?"

"Eh, I think it needs some work. Keep it simple. Do you have any ideas where we can put it?" Kait asks.

"I was thinking we get two printed, a big one that would go across the top of our windshield and a smaller one for the window in the back. I also found a local place that will print them."

After a few revisions to the decal, I send the final version off to the print shop and render out the final video (Here's the video: https://youtu.be/_pclCUcXnds).

"We're going to need to find a place with Wi-Fi and upload the video," I tell Kait.

"Why can't we just upload it using your hotspot like we did the last one?"

"Because we're almost out of data for the month, and we're not even halfway through our billing cycle. We're going to need a larger data plan."

"Well, I don't mind going to a coffee shop," Kait says. "Plus, it would be nice to take a bit of a break from the show. There is a lot of work I need to get done on the website. I'm stressed about the lack of growth, and our revenue is starting to decline."

"That's been stressing me out as well," I tell her. "Our revenue should be growing, not declining. We have seven months to make this work."

The bright side of all this is since our original budget was based on the cost of living in Los Angeles, we've been able to stretch our dollars further outside of California. By cutting our expenses, we can stay on the road longer, giving us more time to figure this out. However, if things don't start growing soon, we're going to burn through our savings.

We drive to a nearby coffee shop, and while I'm getting the video uploaded, Kait gets to work on the website. We've found that by dividing responsibilities, we're no longer getting in each other's hair. I'll review her articles while she reviews my videos, but otherwise we're responsible for our different platforms. Once we're done, we swing by the print shop to pick up our decals. As I'm paying the bill, Kait unrolls the decal for the front window and taps me on the shoulder.

"What's up?" I ask.

"How big did you make this?" She says, with a hint of worry in her voice.

Without turning to look, I say, "Uh, I think I had them make the letters ten inches tall. I was reading that's a good size for signs."

"I think it might be too big."

I turn to see a giant decal that Kait has unrolled across the counter and my stomach drops. "I don't know if that's even going to fit across the front windshield," I say. "Maybe we can put it along the side of the motorhome?"

After staring at it for a moment, Kait and I start laughing at how large the decal is, trying to imagine what it's going to look like on our motorhome. We both shrug it off and decide to put the rear decal on and figure out what to do with this one later.

We don't make it back into the show until one in the afternoon. It's significantly cooler today, so we decide to take Leo with us again. He really enjoyed going around the show yesterday and was excited when we asked if he wanted to go today. I seriously think he understands what we're saying to him, however "come" and "no" aren't in his vocabulary but "food" and "walk" are.

It's midday on a Wednesday, and the show is packed. Our plan for the afternoon is to skip the RVs and spend our time checking out the vendor booths. We saw some cool stuff yesterday that we want to film while the vendors are fresh and excited to show off their products. Having worked a few large trade shows at my previous job, I remember what it felt like on those last days of a show. Your feet are tired, your throat is sore, and all you want to do is pack up and head home.

The first stop we make is the Harvest Hosts booth where we meet the founders of the RV membership program. We let them know how much we enjoy it and ask if we can interview them. They both agree and after a great interview, Kait invites them over for dinner so we can get to know them better and not monopolize their time at the show.

We continue weaving our way through the crowds of people looking for more interesting and innovative products. When we find a product we like and would consider buying,

I interview a representative from the company about what it is they make or do. We figure that it's a great way to introduce people to cool and innovative products they might not be aware of.

By the time we make it through the final hall, it's time for us to head back, clean up the motorhome and get dinner started for our guests. Shortly after the sun sets, we get a knock on the door, and Don and Kim, the owners of Harvest Hosts, present us with a nice bottle of red wine from one of their favorite Hosts. Over dinner, Don and Kim tell us about their adventures overseas and how they took a small motorhome around Europe. We learn that a lot of people ship their small campers to Europe and other parts of the world to expand their adventures beyond North America. Kait and I are fascinated, and I can tell the wheels are turning in her head.

After dinner we say goodnight to our new friends, and I get to work editing our Day Two video. I still have some content left from yesterday that I'm able to weave into today's video to make it a bit more interesting. When it's done, Kait has fewer changes for me than the last one, and we're both very happy with the final product. I feel like I'm beginning to get in a groove with editing these and am finding it to be a lot of fun.

The next morning we decide to head back to our coffee shop. As I'm walking to our table with my coffee, I can tell Kait is very excited about something.

"Guess what!" She exclaims.

"What?

"We're over a hundred subscribers on YouTube and over two-hundred views on our RV Show Day One video! People are even leaving us comments!"

"Seriously?" I say in a mild state of shock. Up until this point, our videos have only gotten a handful of views each day. To get over two-hundred views in one day is amazing. "I wonder how people are finding the video."

"I guess they are searching for the show and our video is showing up in the results."

"That's pretty amazing!" I say, giving Kait a high-five. "Guess I better get to work uploading our Day Two video and respond to those comments!" (Day Two video: https://youtu.be/eO6He4NAvgY)

Knowing that people are watching and enjoying our videos is a big motivation for us. The amount of time we've dedicated to shooting and editing these videos has been increasing. We keep telling ourselves the effort going into the content production is an investment, but I've been having my doubts as to whether or not it will pay off. Although two-hundred views are a tiny blip on the radar, it feels like our content is finally getting out there and gives me a bit of hope that we can, in fact, turn our content production into something that keeps us on the road.

With our work done and excited to make another video, we head back to the motorhome to drop Leo off; however, he has other ideas. As soon as I open the door to the Jeep, he leaps out and begins dragging me towards the entrance of the show.

"Leo!" I exclaim.

Leo stops and turns his head just enough to look at me through the corner of his eye for a moment.

"What? Do you want to go with us?" I ask.

Leo throws his head in the air, giving me a sharp howl and drops down onto his front legs. It's zoomie time, something every husky owner knows well. About once a day, Leo goes into this crazed state where he spins, runs, jumps and tears from one end of the area he's in to another. Since he's on a leash, he can't get far, but that makes what he's doing look even more ridiculous, and I can't help but join him. I charge Leo and give him a giant bear hug, shaking him from side to side. This seems to energize him even more, and we continue to play for a few minutes until we're both out of breath.

With Leo in tow, our strategy today is to film two motorhome walk-throughs requested by our new subscribers. When I checked the comments earlier, there were requests for two specific motorhome models, so we set out to find them at the show. Since we have Leo, only one of us can go in a motorhome at a time, so Kait decides to do the walk-through of the requested Newmar, and I take the Fleetwood.

Afterwards, we start strolling through the show to see if we missed anything of interest. Just past the Sportsmobile display, we see something that catches Kait's eye. "Let's go check out that van," Kait says. Since we've been at the show, she's been gravitating towards the smaller RVs, especially after talking to Don and Kim last night.

"Hymer. Never heard of them," I say.

"We're a German company," one of the representatives says in response. "The Grand Canyon is our North American debut."

"Is it for sale yet?" Kait asks.

"Not yet. This is a concept. We're planning on having it in showrooms mid-year."

"Which chassis is this?" I ask.

"It's the Ram ProMaster. Front-wheel drive which allows the van to have a much lower floor than those with rear-wheel drive."

"Do you mind showing me around the Hymer while I film you?"

"Not at all."

Walking into the Hymer, we see that the interior is quite different than many of the Class B vans we've seen so far. It has a European look and feel. Everything seems modern, clean and functional. The front area of the van looks like a small living room. Both driver and passenger seats turn around to face a fold-out table with a bench seat on the other side. There is a full kitchen with a two-burner gas stove, small bathroom and fairly large bed. The rep explains that the bed folds up when you're not using it so you can store a kayak, bike or something else in the back. There is also quite a bit of storage under either side of the bed.

"I really like this," Kait says from the driver's seat that's turned around.

"This is really nice," I respond. "This is the first van I've seen that I can actually see us living in."

"Me too!" Kait says grabbing my arm. "Think of all the places we could go in something this small. I love our Newmar, but I feel like it's too big for us. How many times have we passed something up because we wouldn't fit or were worried about getting stuck? Plus, how amazing would it be to go around Europe in a camper van?"

"It would be pretty amazing, but we could still get stuck in this. Since we saw the Winnebago View the other day, I've actually been thinking about how feasible it would be for us to live in something smaller."

"I think we could do it," Kait says, standing up and walking into the bathroom. She sits down on the toilet and says, "Look, there is a shower in here, toilet and sink. What else do we need?"

"You're right, but are you suggesting we sell our motorhome and get a van?"

"I don't know, but I'd like to look at some other vans and see what else is available."

"Okay, why don't we spend the rest of our day looking at vans."

When we bought our Newmar, it was small compared to other motorhomes we were looking at. At one point we were seriously considering a diesel pusher no smaller than thirty-eight feet. The reason we were looking at such large rigs was because we felt we needed the space for both dogs. Now that we only have Leo, our space requirements have changed. It's made us look at the way we travel differently and realize that something smaller might be better for us.

After the Hymer the layouts of the other vans we look at are all very similar. Most are built on the Mercedes Sprinter chassis with a couch in the back that converts into a bed at night and are about thirty thousand dollars more expensive than the Hymer.

"What did you think about that one?" I ask Kait as she walks out of another Mercedes conversion.

"It's nice, but it looks like the last one we saw. I don't like the idea of having to make the bed every night since it doubles as the couch. I like that the Grand Canyon has a permanent bed in the back with a living room area up front."

"So do I, but I don't think we could live in it full-time."

"Why not?" Kait asks.

"Where would we put all of our stuff?" I ask. Before Kait has a chance to respond I continue, "I agree that we can get rid of some of our stuff, but in the van we wouldn't even have enough room for all our clothes, let alone any of the other things we have. We'd literally have to get rid of everything we have stored in the bays, plus about half of what we have stored inside the motorhome."

"Well it's something to think about," Kait says. "I could do it, but I know you like having your stuff. I'm very excited to go through everything in the motorhome and start getting rid of stuff. Even if we don't get something smaller, at least we can declutter our lives."

Kait is definitely a minimalist and when she says she can do it, I believe her. I, on the other hand, as Kait so rightly pointed out, like my stuff. It was a struggle for me to downsize from our 1,250-square-foot home to the motorhome. I agonized over things like which tools to bring and what to sell. I loaded as much as I could into the motorhome and still felt like I didn't have everything I wanted. Now that we've been on the road, I realize there are many things I brought that we never use. I'm reminded of it every time I have to unpack an entire bay just to grab something I'm looking for.

In that sense I'm also excited about the idea of getting rid of things, but I don't see any way we could downsize enough to fit our lives into a van.

The next few days are spent checking out other small motorhomes, a couple trailers and more of the vendor booths. The show is absolutely packed on Saturday, and we notice the crowd has gone from mainly retired couples to families with children. It's wall-to-wall people and has become too crowded to film any thing else, so we head back to the motorhome to get work done. That night a heavy thunderstorm rolls through, and when I open the door Sunday morning, I find that we're now camped in the middle of a small lake.

"We're going to have to move," I tell Kait. "There's a good six to eight inches of water out there. There are a few sites that are on higher ground where can move."

Heading back outside, I trudge through the ice cold water to unplug our electrical cord, being very careful not to electrocute myself. It's still raining, so by the time I'm done and get the motorhome moved, I'm soaking wet and cold. Kait suggests I take a shower and has already fired up the water heater, so it's ready to go. I love that woman. When I get into the shower, I'm so cold that the warm water is sending pins and needles through my toes and fingers, but I feel a hundred times better.

Standing under the hot water, I can't stop thinking about the vans we saw yesterday. I like the idea of the Winnebago View. It's larger with more storage, on the Mercedes chassis and could tow our Jeep. The downside is that it's still larger than a standard parking spot and we'd have many of the same problems in terms of size that we have now. I like the Hymer, but it doesn't have the capacity to tow the Jeep and rather than a black tank it has a four-and-a-half gallon cassette toilet that we'd have to empty every couple days. There are a lot of options but none that seem practical with our current lifestyle.

What am I thinking? Sure, it's exciting that our videos are picking up, but unless some miracle happens in the next seven months, we'll be looking for jobs rather than a smaller RV.

"Why don't we take today off," Kait suggests when I walk out of the bathroom.

"And skip the show?"

"It's raining and I figure we need a break. Let's go do something fun!"

"What do you have in mind?"

"Well, there is a Thai temple nearby that has a Sunday market, and they serve food. It's cash only, but I was reading that the food is amazing, and people start lining up before it's even open. If that sounds good..."

"I'm in," I respond, cutting Kait off. "Thai food sounds great, and I have plenty of cash. Let me just make a cup of coffee for the drive."

The temple is a short drive from the fairgrounds. We arrive ten minutes before they start serving food, but the parking lot is already over half full, and I can see people lined up at various stalls. The rain has let up a bit, but it's unusually cold out. The food must be good for so many people to come out in this weather.

Walking up to the temple, we see multiple stalls, each serving a different type of food. Sweets, curries, noodle soups, and there is a large vat of oil for frying something. "Let's get in the soup line first," Kait suggests.

According to reviews, the noodle soup is one of the most popular dishes at the market and has the longest line. They haven't started serving soup yet, so we grab a combo of pumpkin and massaman curry to snack on while we wait. By the time we queue up for soup, there are about twenty people ahead of us, and even with our snack, I'm starving. My saving grace is that I still have half a tumbler of piping hot coffee to enjoy while we wait.

"Honey!" Kait says excitedly, looking at her phone. "We're almost at 200 YouTube subscribers!"

"Already? We just hit a hundred the other day. I can't believe we're growing that quickly."

"I know; covering the show has really helped us. From the comments I'm reading, people seem to enjoy the walkthrough videos."

"Interesting. Maybe we should consider doing more of those and putting the vlogs on hold," I say. "I thought people would be more interested in the travel videos but the RV related content seems to be drawing more of an audience."

"Let's talk about it over noodle soup. We're almost at the front," Kait says, sliding her phone back in her pocket. Despite my arguments against it, Kait only orders one bowl of soup for us to share. She's trying to convince me that there are plenty of other things for us to try and we should save room. I'm not sold on the idea because this soup looks and smells amazing.

Walking back to the Jeep an hour later, I concede that Kait was right about the soup. While it tasted even better than it looked, our culinary adventures didn't end there. After an order of pork skewers, Kait spotted these vats of bubbling oil and a woman dropping in chunks of banana covered in some sort of batter. Grabbing my arm, Kait dragged me into a line that was growing faster than our subscribers.

A woman ahead of us in line suggested when we order that we ask for extra crispies. "Trust me," she said. We had no idea what that meant, but we followed her advice. When we ordered, the woman collecting money grabbed a paper bag and began shoveling fried bananas into it. Once she'd filled it, she shoveled another couple scoops of these little nuggets into the bag which turned out to be batter that had dripped into the oil and fried into golden perfection, a.k.a. the crispies.

Opening up the door to the Jeep, I pull myself inside. It feels like I've gained ten pounds in the last hour and I'm in desperate need of a nap. "Do you want another banana?" Kait asks, more interested in the crispies.

"Okay," I respond. As full as I am, these things are just too good.

I had the foresight to film our experience at the temple, so when we get back to the motorhome I start putting together our next vlog. My hope is that we can capitalize on all of our new subscribers and entice them to watch our vlog style videos (Video from the Thai Temple: https://youtu.be/3GI56A4zofU).

Monday morning the show is over, and everyone is packing up. As we're driving out of the fairgrounds, I look over at the large grass field we saw when we first pulled in. With everyone leaving today and the rain, the field has turned into a giant mud pit with cars and motorhomes stuck in various positions. There are a couple of those giant tow trucks they use for semi-trucks, pulling motorhomes free.

We take in the scene in silence before Kait says, "I'm so happy we didn't end up camping out there."

"It's going to take a long time to get everyone out," I say as we leave the fairgrounds.

"I really enjoyed the show, but I'm ready for a few days off," Kait says.

"Me too."

16. "SPRING" CLEANING

Friday, January 22nd, 2016

"Can we take some time while we're at the campground to go through the motorhome and do some spring cleaning?" Kait asks. We're on our way to an RV resort to take a few days off after the show. We've been moving and seeing a lot, so we figured spending a week in one place with no distractions would be good for us. I agree, but Kait isn't the only one who has plans for our time off. I have a few minor things to fix around the motorhome. I need to install a vent cover we ordered and get our giant We're the Russos decal put on.

Kait's excited for spring cleaning. She wants to show me that we can get rid of enough stuff to justify moving to a smaller RV. The more I think about it, the less I think it's a possibility. On paper it seems like a great idea. Get something small that we can take just about anywhere and live out of that. The reality is, we're going to be on top of each other in such a small space. The bathrooms are tiny and in most cases are wet baths (toilet and shower in the same space), and our tanks will be so small we'll only be able to boondock for a few days before we have to find a place to dump. I don't think Kait's thought all of this through, but I'm happy to take some time to get rid of things we no longer need.

"Are you okay to drive in this?" Kait asks. The rain is coming down so hard I've had to slow down significantly.

"I think so. I just have to focus on the road until we get to the RV resort."

At the park, we pull up to the RV parking area next to the main office. I go in to get us checked in while Kait detaches the Jeep.

"Good afternoon," the woman behind the counter says, as I walk through the door. "It looks like the rain stopped just in time for y'all."

"Yeah, it was a bit rough driving over here from the Tampa area, but we made it."

"Well, Mr. Russo, I have your reservation here. Let me just show you where your site is on the map." The woman places a map of the park on the counter in front of me. "We're right here," she says, circling the main office with a black marker. "Take this road, then make a right," she says, plotting our course in black ink. "Once you get to the end of the street, you'll drive into the field, coming in behind your spot so you can pull straight in."

The woman turns the map around to me. She's traced the route out on the map so I can follow it. The first time someone did this for us during our stay at an RV park in Gainesville, I dismissed their route, opting for one that seemed to be more direct. I quickly realized that the person in the front office knows a lot more about their park than I do, and it's no fun backing a twenty-nine-foot motorhome down a narrow road you weren't supposed to go down in the first place. So when I am told to drive around behind our site, that's exactly what I intend to do.

"Follow me to the site?" I ask Kait.

"Yep, Leo and I will be right behind you in the Jeep. Don't pull into the site until I can get out and back you in."

"No need. The woman told me to drive in behind the site and pull straight into it."

Driving down the road, I see that our site is at the end of a cul-de-sac. To the right of it is the dirt road that leads into the field. The cul-de-sac is very narrow, so I understand why they ask people to drive around behind the sites to pull in rather than trying to maneuver a large motorhome in this tight area.

The dirt road seems a bit wet from the rain but doesn't appear to be muddy, so I continue on. The road fades into a field of grass, which I drive onto and make the turn towards our site. As I drive further onto the grass, I realize this was a mistake. The field has a bit of a depression and is flooded from the rainstorm. The water isn't deep, but I can feel our 20,000-pound motorhome getting sluggish and the rear wheels starting to spin as I encourage the motorhome forward with the gas pedal.

I should have turned around before I drove onto the grass, but if I stop now, we'll have to get towed out. Regardless, the field is so saturated with water that I think I may get stuck anyway. Scenes from the field at the RV show with the large tow trucks come flying into my head, and for a moment, I wonder if I should just let up on the gas and wait for the field to dry out.

I make the decision to go for it. I'm only about fifty feet from the site, so I start pumping the gas pedal, trying to keep the momentum up. Every time I press the gas, I can feel the rear wheels spin, but I'm managing to keep the motorhome moving forward. As I get closer to the concrete pad, I see another obstacle. There is a large mud pit just before the site where it seems an unlucky soul may have gotten stuck and spun their tires.

I continue pumping the gas pedal, trying to build up some momentum to make it through the mud then over the lip of the concrete pad. As soon as my front wheels hit the mud, the motorhome slows down drastically and I feel the front wheels hit the edge of the pad. I'm thrown slightly off my seat as the wheels clear the lip and are on solid concrete. Unfortunately, this used up most of the motorhome's momentum and pressing the gas pedal now does nothing. It feels like my rear tires are on ice, but the motorhome is still moving forward. I keep pumping the gas trying to get some bite, but it seems to make no difference. Inch by inch, the motorhome continues to creep forward. At any moment I expect to stop, but the motorhome keeps going. Just as the motorhome is about to come to a stop, I give the gas pedal one last push and feel the rear wheels dig into the edge of the concrete pad and pull the motorhome onto the pad. I made it!

Once I'm able to relax, I realize sweat is pouring down my face and I see Kait standing alongside the pad with a look of shock on her face.

"What happened? Why did you go drive through the field?" Kait asks in an upset and confused tone.

"That's what the woman at the front desk told me to do. Once I got on the grass, I couldn't turn around so I just kept going. Next time I'll get out and walk around before trying something like that."

"Well, good job on not getting stuck," Kait says with a much softer tone. "You should come outside and see the mess you made."

Walking outside, I see that the entire rear of the motorhome is covered in mud. Mud is packed between the rear dual rear wheels and has been thrown all over the rear overhang of the motorhome. Looking back into the field, I can see where the wheels first started spinning by the ruts I left in the mud. I'm shocked I managed to get onto the pad.

"I'll grab the hose and spray all of this down," I tell Kait. "If that mud dries, we'll never get it out."

"Okay, you do that, and I'll get us set up inside. Good luck!"

"Thanks," I reply, shaking my head.

Hooking up the hose to the spigot at our site, I wash off the mud thinking that this is another lesson learned. Before we hit the road, I read articles on how to properly drive a motorhome; watched videos on YouTube and found just about every piece of advice I could. They gave me a good base of knowledge, but nothing compared to what I've learned since we hit the road.

"Don't get too close to other cars when making a turn because the rear overhang can swing out into the lane next to you," was one piece of advice I read in an article. That's all well and good until someone in the lane next to you decides to stop inches from the side of your rig. Now what? I thought I knew everything there was to know, but I'm continually humbled by all there is to learn and experience. Oh, and if you're now wondering what to do if said person does stop inches from you when you need to make that turn...my suggestion is to pull far enough forward that the rear of the motorhome is past the front of the car, or simply wait for them to drive off. You might be holding traffic up, but I've learned that it's better to be honked at than cause a wreck. The key is to take your time and be patient.

It's still raining when we get up in the morning, so Kait and I decide to catch up on work for the day. Since the Tampa show, we've continued to grow, both in subscribers and revenue from the ads we have on our website and those in our YouTube videos. In December we made a total of $49. This month we've already made $70, and we still have a week to go. If things continue, we may double our income this month, which would be incredible considering that a week ago we were stressed that our website revenue was declining.

I've turned the front of the motorhome into my edit bay. The passenger seat has a desk that pulls out and allows me to work comfortably, while having the large front window to look out of. When I have my headphones on, I feel like this is my own private office. A nice luxury when living in a small space.

Sunday, January 24th, 2016

"It's nice out and I want to get our spring cleaning done today," Kait says, nudging me awake.

"What time is it?" I ask.

"Just after eight. I'll make you coffee if you get up."

She knows me too well. "Start the water then, I'm up."

Our plan for the day is simple. Go through every drawer, closet, bay and container we have in the motorhome and get rid of things we haven't used. When we first got on the road, we said that if we didn't use something the first six months, we'd get rid of it. It's only been five months since we hit the road but six months since we moved in, so it's time to purge.

We decided to start in the bedroom. With coffee in hand, I sit on the floor and start going through my drawers. There are six total. I have two, Kait has two and we've kind of split the other two. My top drawer is stuffed with socks and underwear. "Do you think I'll need these?" I ask holding up a pair of dress socks.

"Well, do you plan to wear the dress shoes in the closet?" Kait asks.

"Probably not. Okay, all of these can go," I say pulling out a few more pairs. "I still have no idea where my ankle socks are. I know I brought them, but I have no idea where they ended up.

"And you're sure they're not buried at the bottom of your sock drawer?"

"Yep, nothing," I say, lifting everything up to show her.

Moving onto the bottom drawer, I find some winter clothes I'd forgotten about. A couple light sweaters, long underwear and some exercise clothes. I pull a few items out that I don't plan to wear, tossing them into the donation pile we've started. Meanwhile, Kait has pulled the entire contents of her closet out and is making piles on the bed. After she inspects each item, it either ends up in a growing pile to her left or gets placed back in the closet. The majority of clothes aren't making it back into the closet. Watching her is fascinating, so I sit back with my coffee to enjoy the show.

"Why are you getting rid of that?" I ask, referring to a red button-down blouse.

"Because I haven't worn it. I'm getting rid of anything I haven't worn while we've been on the road. It's nice, but I don't need it," Kait says with a smile. "There's no use holding onto things I no longer need. It's just been sitting at the bottom of my closet taking up room, so I'm letting it go."

Finished with my coffee, I move on to my closet and, taking a cue from Kait, pull everything out and lay it on the bed. When we moved in, we decided that rather than hanging everything in our closets, we'd fold and stack our clothes. As I go through the stack, I realize that I've simply been picking clothes off the top and haven't touched anything at the bottom. Every time I put clean clothes away, they go on top of the pile. Going forward, I'm going to take the clean clothes and put them at the bottom of the pile so I can rotate through everything. While I'm not nearly as liberal at getting rid of things, about a quarter of what I pulled out doesn't make it back into the closet.

"Look what I found," Kait says with a laugh. I turn to see her holding up all of my missing ankle socks.

"Where did you find those?"

"Right here," she says, laughing and pointing to one of the shared drawers. "In six months you haven't even opened this drawer!" She opens my sock drawer and consolidates what she's found into it. "Okay, these two middle drawers are now empty."

This process continues as we progress toward the front of the motorhome. Each time we pull the contents of a cabinet or drawer out, we find things we've been looking for or have forgotten about. When we first packed the motorhome, I was insistent that we bring as much as possible. I felt like we had to try and replicate our lives in a sticks-and-bricks house in the motorhome. I had no idea what we would need and what we wouldn't, so I figured we bring it all and sort it out later. Well, about half the stuff we brought is going either in the donation or the trash pile.

"You know, the one thing I wish we hadn't gotten rid of when we moved in was our slow cooker," Kait says as she puts the remaining two pots and one pan away. "It'd be really nice if we could put a meal together and set it to cook while we're out or driving to our next destination so we have a hot meal when we arrive."

"Why don't we go buy one?" I ask.

"Because we don't need it. I just said it'd be nice to have."

"Alright, but if you'd like to get one we have more than enough room for it now."

"What would we get rid of?" Kait asks. Kait made me agree to the one-in-one-out rule. So, for example, if I were to buy a new shirt, I would have to get rid of one.

"You're right, but if you change your mind, I'm sure we can find something to get rid of."

"What do you think, Leo?" Kait asks in a playful tone.

He looks up at Kait from his spot under the steering wheel where he's been supervising our progress. Crawling out from his spot, he stretches, lets out a snort and spins around, dropping on his front legs.

"Uh oh, I think someone is ready for a walk." I say. Leo spins again and does a little hop towards the door. "Okay, let's take you for a walk, and then we can get started on the bays."

We always love walking through RV parks to see everyone's set-up. This park is a bit different. Many of the people here are snowbirds and have seasonal sites while others live here year round. A few have an RV of some type that they bring down each winter but most have what's known as a park model. Park models are trailers designed to be a more permanent setup, similar to a mobile home. Some look like they've been here for quite a while, and others appear to be brand new. A few people even have decks and outdoor patios built around their sites.

"I can't believe how much stuff we're getting rid of," I say.

"Oh, I can, and I feel like we can get rid of even more," Kait says in response. "I could probably get rid of half the clothes I decided to keep, and we really don't need things like the extra bedding or the extra sets of glasses and utensils."

"True, but they're nice to have in case we ever have people over," I counter.

"We've been on the road for six months, and John is the only person who's come to visit. Everyone said they would but he was the only person who flew out, and even then he stayed in a hotel. Would you want people staying with us in the motorhome?"

"Not for more than a night. It'd be too cramped. Plus I feel like they'd have a hard time adapting to the bathroom."

"Exactly. And when we have people come over for dinner or drinks, we can just ask them to bring their own glasses, plates and utensils. As we've learned, it's good RV etiquette to bring your own anyway."

"You make a good point," I say. "I hadn't really thought of that. If we got rid of all the extra stuff we've kept for guests plus what we've already pulled out, half of the storage in the motorhome is going to be empty."

"At least!" Kait says, slapping my arm. "I feel so liberated and want to get rid of more stuff. I can't wait to go through the bays."

After a loop around the park, Leo leads us back to the motorhome. It's sunny so he plops down under the picnic table to enjoy a nap on the cool concrete while we get to work. Each bay is opened and emptied. Every item is scrutinized and either returned to the bay or set aside to be sold, donated or tossed.

The night before the new owners took possession of our house, we still had quite a few things in the garage. Most were thrown out, but not before I packed as much as I could into what little empty space we had left. I felt this need to stuff our motorhome to the gills. Now I just shake my head, wondering what I was thinking. These things have just been weighing us down, literally, and taking up space for no other reason than because I found an empty nook or two I wanted to fill. Each time we drive the motorhome, we're paying to drag that excess stuff around with us. The reduction in weight might make a very small difference at the gas pump, but when we're only getting seven MPG, every bit counts.

"Do we need all of these extension cords and surge protectors?" Kait asks, pointing to a pile she's made.

"Nope. Let's just hold onto the fifty-foot orange cord, and we can get rid of the rest. We have a surge protector for the motorhome, so we don't need any of those for the outlets. We can also toss the cans of spray paint and the big bottles of cleansers. We don't wash our windows all that often so we don't need an industrial sized bottle of window cleaner."

The only bay that we don't clean much out of is my tool bay. Although I haven't used most of the tools since we hit the road, we agree that it's better to hold onto them and not need them, than need them and not have them, especially since we have the room.

By the time we're finished, we have a substantial pile of things that we've packed into the back of the Jeep to take to a donation center. Aside from a few small items, nothing is worth selling. We know we can get rid of more but this was a good first step towards downsizing.

A smaller RV is now starting to look like more of a reality than some crazy idea.

17. EXPECT THE UNEXPECTED

Tuesday, February 16th, 2016

A siren rings out. I shoot up in bed, looking around the room, but it's pitch black. Where am I? Light flashes around the edges of the window shades and I hear a loud crack close by. I can't focus. It sounds like all hell is breaking loose outside of the motorhome.

"What is it? What's going on?" Kait asks in a panic.

"I don't know. I think some kind of warning came through your phone. What's it say?"

"Uh, hold on." Kait turns on the light next to her bed and picks up her phone. "It's a severe weather warning. 'Be advised, severe thunderstorm warning in effect. Winter storms with possible tornados until 2 a.m.'"

Getting out of bed, I throw my clothes on and run to the front of the motorhome. Bringing the front shade up, I see lightning coming down all around us and sideways rain. The rain is hitting the side of our neighbor's motorhome so hard, it looks like there is a jet of water coming off the top. Lightning flashes about two-hundred yards from us and the boom shakes the motorhome, sending Leo for cover under the steering wheel.

"I'm scared," Kait says. She's sitting in bed, with the covers wrapped around herself. "What are we going to do?"

I haven't had time to process everything. Taking a breath I look at her and say, "Everything will be okay. Get dressed and let's figure out what's going on."

The walkie-talkies we own also have a NOAA weather station we can tune into, so I grab one and set it up while Kait gets dressed. Turning it on, an eerie-sounding electronic voice announces that there is a severe thunderstorm coming through that will affect the area until 8 a.m. The voice then goes on to say that there is a tornado watch until 5:30 a.m. Looking at my phone, I see it's 4:33 a.m.

After our experience with the flash flood warning in Pagosa Springs, Colorado, we put together a plan if anything like that should happen again. Kait is in charge of packing our bug out bags. We have everything ready to go in smaller, separate bags, so all she has to do is throw them in our backpacks. We always keep at least one full case of drinking water in the back of the Jeep and spare food in case we ever get stranded while off-roading. My job is to figure out what the situation is, get Leo's harness on in case we have to carry him and prep the Jeep.

"This is hotel security," a shaky voice says over the phone.

"Hi, we're staying in an RV in the parking lot and were wondering if we could come inside the casino with our dog if a tornado touches down in the area?" I ask.

"Absolutely. You're welcome to come in now or whenever you want."

"Thanks. Has a tornado ever touched down around here?" I ask.

"No, but we've never seen it this bad."

When we pulled into the casino a couple nights ago, we thought this would be the perfect place to spend a few days. Hard to believe we were sitting outside enjoying a drink with the neighbors yesterday and now we're getting ready to abandon our home if necessary.

At 4:40 a.m., Kait hands me the two bags she packed, and I press the unlock button on the Jeep's key fob. Through the wall of rain, I can barely make out the flash of the Jeep's lights indicating the doors are now unlocked.

"Be careful," Kait says, putting her hand on my shoulder. I have to force the door to the motorhome open. There are sustained winds of over forty miles per hour, and when I step outside, I'm blinded by the rain. It's hitting me straight in the face as I run towards the Jeep.

Whipping the driver's door open, I throw the bags into the passenger seat and jump in. In the ten seconds it took me to run to the Jeep, my clothes are completely soaked through. I have my rain coat on but the water managed to get under it and soak my shirt. Sitting in the driver's seat, I take another breath and wipe my glasses off. This is the first moment I've had to think about what's going on. Looking across the parking lot, I realize I can't even see the hotel and casino through the heavy downpour. There could be a tornado on the other side of this parking lot and we'd never know until it was right on top of us. I'm scared. Storms don't scare me but there is something different about this one.

Starting the Jeep, I back out of the parking spot and pull alongside our motorhome. If we do need to get out, I want the Jeep right here, ready to go. I'd like to go over to the casino now, but, due to Leo's fear of going in buildings, we'd have to drag or carry him inside. I had to do that when we visited a friend in Colorado, and it took Leo a few weeks to trust that we weren't going to try and drag him in another building. I don't want a repeat of that if we can help it. On top of that, he's completely freaked out by this storm, and I don't want to compound the issue.

"You're soaking wet. Why don't you put some dry clothes on," Kait says, handing me a towel when I walk back inside.

"Thanks, the Jeep is all ready to go."

"Okay, but I don't want to take Leo into the casino unless we have to," Kait says.

"I was just thinking the same thing."

After I finish putting my clothes on, I notice it's gotten very quiet. My heart starts beating and I feel more adrenaline pumping through my veins. The jet engine sound from the wind and rain has suddenly stopped and that scares me.

Walking back outside, I look up and see a sky full of stars. There are still some scattered clouds but the sky is clear. It's like the storm was never here. "Do you think it's over?" Kait asks from the doorway of the motorhome.

Without turning around, I yell back, "I don't think so. I think we're in the eye of the storm."

I'd always heard about what it's like to be in the eye and I find it oddly calming. Logically, I know this is only a temporary respite. However, the other side of my brain is trying to convince me that things are over.

"I think it's going to get worse," I tell Kait as I walk back in the motorhome.

"Well, it's almost 5. The tornado watch should be ending. Maybe it's over?"

"Maybe."

It's unsettling being in weather like this with the motorhome, especially having such a thin roof. During a normal rainstorm, you can hear every drop, and I find it soothing. However, in weather like this, the storm reminds you that all that's between you and it is the thin skin of the motorhome.

I hear a buzzing from my phone, then Kait's phone goes off again. Picking it up, I see another alert. "Tornado warning in this area until 5 a.m. Eastern Time. Take shelter now. Check local media."

Kait is sitting in the driver's seat, which is currently turned around facing the living room. She is looking from side to side frantically, trying to see if she can see anything. At that moment, the wind picks up again and is worse than before. A few seconds later, the rain begins, and I can see flashes of light approaching.

Kait grabs her phone and opens the weather app. We've been keeping close tabs on the weather, but we'd found that storms in Florida can come out of nowhere. There was a slight chance of rain when she checked yesterday but nothing to be worried about. "I'm checking NOAA and the National Weather Service on Twitter," Kait says.

"Why Twitter? Wouldn't you just check the news stations?"

"Because it has realtime updates. The news stations are checking the same feed. Here, look," Kait says, handing me her phone. Looking at it, I see a tweet from one of the weather services.

Confirmed tornado touch down along alligator alley in Collier County. FHP trooper spotted near MM 70 after 5 a.m.

Opening Google Maps, I look at our current location compared to where the tornado was spotted. "We're only about thirty miles north of where it touched down," I tell Kait.

"Okay. According to the satellite view, we're on the northern edge of the storm. It looks like it should pass in about twenty minutes. We should be fine here."

The next twenty minutes are tense as we watch the storm from the windows, but eventually it passes. The rain continues but the storm calmed down significantly. As our nerves began to subside, we were both wiped out from the experience and crawled back into bed as the sun was beginning to come up.

It was a scary night for us and not something we'll soon forget. We didn't feel the least bit secure in our "home," and it's the first time in a long time that I've missed being in a sticks and bricks home. I love the lifestyle we lead, but there is something to be said about having solid walls. Going forward, we'll have to make a mental note to be aware of the locations of tornado shelters.

BONUS CONTENT: Here's a video of our experience during the storm: https://youtu.be/3Bu5MAXxoVM

18. BIG TIME RV

Wednesday, March 16th, 2016

"We just got an email from a production company who's interested in having us on the TV show Big Time RV," Kait says as I'm piloting our motorhome north on Interstate 95 towards Savannah, Georgia. "They want to schedule a Skype call with us and their casting director tomorrow."

"Really?" I ask in amazement. "That's exciting, but if I remember correctly the show is about people who are in the market to buy an RV. I know we've talked about moving to a camper van, but I'm not ready to buy anything."

"Neither am I, but I think we should hear what they have to say. We might not have to buy anything and just pick the one we like the most."

I don't know if I would want to be on a TV show. While I'm open to talking to them, I have my concerns. I know how real reality TV works and who knows how we might come across once the show is edited. Since we posted our first vlog in December, we've continued to make videos and will be posting vlog number twenty-seven in a few days. Any stage fright I had when we started has long since dissipated, but there is something about being on an actual TV show that is making me very nervous. Regardless, I can see how excited Kait is, so I tell her to schedule a call for tomorrow.

My fear and anxiousness are soon replaced with excitement during our call as the casting director describes how the show will be shot. He's watched some of our YouTube videos and, if we're picked to be on the show, wants us to just be ourselves. He also tells us that we're not under any obligation to purchase an RV. However, if we are interested in the one we pick, we're more than welcome to speak to the salesperson about making a purchase. There is one catch. Filming is scheduled to start in two weeks and we would have to drive back to Tampa. Although they don't know what the lineup will be, we're told that the episode would air later this year.

After spending the last few months in Florida, our plan is to continue up the east coast until early May, then turn west to Indiana for an appointment at Newmar to get some warranty items taken care of. Heading back south to Tampa would throw off our entire plan of driving up the coast.

Nothing is set in stone, and the casting director says it may be a few days until we find out if they want us. I'm still not 100% sold on the idea. So rather than turning around, we decide to continue towards Savannah. If the casting director decides he wants us on the show, we can always turn around and head south.

Just south of Savannah, we pull into a huge flea market that allows RVers to stay overnight as part of the Harvest Hosts program. Kait called yesterday to ask if we could stay and they told us we'd be more than welcome. There is a large field behind the market where we can park anywhere we want for the night.

After we find a nice patch of grass, well away from the handful of other RVs in the field, we take Leo for a long walk around the grounds. He's usually pretty worn out after a long day's drive, but today is an exception. Although it's warm and humid, he's excited to walk around and sniff every rodent burrow he can find, and in this field, they are endless.

With Leo tuckered out, we take him back to the motorhome and head into the flea market to see what interesting things they have. There are a lot of vendors selling cheap electronics and accessories, but a few have some cool Americana on display. Since we've been focused on downsizing, there isn't anything we want to pick up, so we head over to the food stands and grab a few things to "pay" for our stay. Although we can park for free, the expectation is that we make a purchase in exchange.

The next morning I roll over to see Kait sitting in bed, phone in hand looking very excited.

"What's going on?" I ask in a groggy voice.

The casting director emailed us to say they want us to be on the show. They can't pay us to be on the show, but said they'll cover the cost of our campground, reimburse us for the gas to get down there and include shots of our WereTheRussos.com sticker on the RV. They want to start filming on the 31st and Kait is waiting for me to tell her what I think.

I agree with Kait that this could be good exposure for us. Despite my nerves, it's something I'm seriously considering. My concern is that we haven't committed to selling our RV and downsizing to something smaller. I don't want us to go on the show, talk about downsizing, and never do it.

Kait listens as I explain my concerns and she makes the point that regardless of whether it's a camper van or something else, she wants to downsize. That said, ever since we did our spring cleaning I've been thinking more and more about going small. Whenever we're driving someplace in the motorhome, I fantasize about not having to deal with something so large. I just want to make sure that we don't paint ourselves into a corner and realize later that we're happy with what we have.

Kait makes the point that even if we don't downsize, she doesn't think it's a problem. We always have the right to change our minds.

"You make a good point," I say. "Sign me up."

Thursday, March 31st, 2016

Last night I knocked on a couple of our neighbors' doors at the campground asking if anyone had an iron. I can't remember the last time I ironed anything, but I figured being on a TV show was a good excuse to look my best.

"It's going to be hot today," Kait says. "Let's put the AC on before we leave so Leo is comfortable. I checked the schedule they sent us, and we'll have a break at lunch, so we can come back and take him for a walk."

"Sounds good, but I wish I could wear shorts. It's going to be hot in these pants but that's what they said I have to wear," I say as I finish buttoning up my freshly ironed shirt. "How do I look?"

"Really good, honey. It's supposed to cool down a bit tomorrow, so we just need to get through today."

At 8:45 a.m., Nicole, one of the show's production assistants, pulls up to our site in a golf cart. "Good morning, Russos," she says as she walks up to the door. "Ready to get going? We have some paperwork for you to fill out, and then we're going to start shooting."

"We're ready," Kait says as she walks down the stairs of our motorhome. I set the thermostat to sixty-five degrees for Leo. It's been in the mid-eighties since we've been in Florida with ninety-percent humidity, so he's happy to spend the day inside with the AC blowing.

The production company has commandeered one of the used fifth wheels the dealership has on their lot to use as a production office. When we walk in, we're greeted by the crew and handed a couple clipboards with our paperwork to fill out. "Ready to sign your life away?" I joke to Kait.

She smiles back and says, "I don't know about that, but I'm willing to sign the release."

"Hey, Russos, I'm Scott, the producer and director of the show. Here's how it's going to work. We have three Class B RVs picked out for you to look at with a salesman. We'll shoot the three of you going through each RV and your reactions. We want you to forget the cameras are there and just go through them like you normally would. Be yourselves. Occasionally we might ask you to talk more about something or what your thoughts are if we think it might be interesting."

"Sounds good," I say as I finish signing my release.

"I also wanted to ask if we could get some shots of you two in your current RV working, cooking and some shots of your dog?"

"Absolutely. When do you want to do that?"

"We're going to film you going through the vans today and grab the shots of your RV tomorrow. Afterwards we'd like to get some shots of you driving off in whichever van you pick."

"Okay, but we don't actually have to buy it, do we?" Kait asks with a bit of concern in her voice.

"Not at all," Scott responds. "We're just going to get some shots of you stating which van you chose and then a few shots of the two driving down the road. By the way, we've gotten a lot of people on this show who have a small RV and want to go bigger, but you two are the first who actually want to go smaller."

"Something smaller just makes more sense for us with how we like to travel. Plus we might ship it over to Europe one day and do some traveling there," I tell Scott.

"Well I envy you both. Alright, are you two ready to do this?"

"We are," Kait and I say, handing our clipboards back to Nicole.

The dealership is huge, and Nicole drives us over to the area where they have the three RVs we're going to look at. As we drive up, I see a Winnebago Travato, Era and Fuse. The first two are Class B camper vans that we've looked at in the past. The Fuse is a small Class C, similar to the Winnebago View we saw at the Tampa show. It's larger than what we've been considering but might be an interesting option to consider.

"Joe, Kait, I'd like you to meet Livorno, who's going to be your salesman today," Scott says, introducing a gentleman who's walked over to join the crew.

"Joe and Kait Russo, very nice to meet you both. I think we're going to have a lot of fun today," Livorno says, extending his hand. Livorno has a very warm personality with a big smile, and I can see why he's been chosen to be on the show several times in the past. He asks us a few questions about what we're looking for and why we want to switch from our Class A motorhome to a Class B van. He's just as perplexed about our decision as everyone else we've talked to but seems very interested.

The crew has set up around the Era, and we're told that they are ready for us. The Era is the most expensive van out of the three but one we're very interested in. We've looked at these before and it, along with the Hymer we saw, is one of our favorites in this class. It's just over twenty-four feet long on the Mercedes-Benz Sprinter diesel chassis. We like the idea of having a diesel since they tend to get into the mid to high teens for gas mileage and have a higher towing capacity. We're not sure if we want to sell the Jeep and the Sprinter would give us the option to tow it if we did decide to keep it.

I open the sliding door to the Era and am hit with a blast of hot air. The Era they picked is black and has been sitting in the sun with all of the windows closed. The inside feels like an oven. "Let's turn the AC on," Livorno says.

"Great idea," I say. "I'll open the windows and turn the vent on to try and cool it down if you want to get the AC going."

A few minutes later, Livorno and I are dripping with sweat when we step back outside. "Sorry guys but we're going to need to turn the AC off when we start filming," the sound guy says to us as he's looking down at this equipment. "The mics are going to pick up all of that ambient noise."

I'm not surprised, but the heat is going to make it difficult to spend a lot of time in these vans. Looking over, I see Kait sitting in the shade with an ice cold bottle of water on her neck. If she's this hot now, she's not going to be happy when we start shooting.

"We're ready," the camera guy says to Scott.

"Okay. Livorno, I'm going to have you drive over in the golf cart with Joe and Kait. The three of you will walk up to the Era, Livorno will tell you all about it and then take you inside to look around. Any questions?" We all shake our heads and head over to the golf cart.

Every now and again we're asked to reshoot a scene but overall things are progressing fairly quickly. Shooting inside the Era proves to be difficult given the narrow confines of the van, especially because there are four of us inside. Kait, Livorno and I are continually shifting so the cameraman can get the right angle to get the shot. He shoots a wide angle of us looking at the refrigerator, for example, and then gets what he calls "cutaway shots." These are close-up shots of one of us opening a latch or turning some knob.

At first I find the filming process to be very tedious and am getting a bit frustrated each time we have to stop and reshoot something or get the cutaways. However, as we continue to move through the van, I begin to see how they plan to stitch all of the shots together and how the cutaways are going to provide nice transition shots when we're opening or operating something within the RV. I begin to take mental notes as I watch how the cameraman works through each shot, and I think about how we can adopt these techniques to our videos.

We have to keep the doors and windows closed while we're shooting to keep any exterior sound out and the heat builds quickly. In between shots, Livorno or I turn the AC back on, even if it's just for a minute. Depending on where we're standing, one of us will start the engine to run the dash AC and the other will turn on the ceiling unit in the back of the van. The crew has grabbed towels for everyone so we can wipe ourselves off whenever we're stopped for a second. My towel's already soaking wet.

"Alright everyone, let's break for lunch," Scott says as we get the final shots of the Era. "We'll pick up with the Fuse when we come back. Joe, Kait, we picked up some sandwiches for you at Publix if you'd like them."

"Absolutely," we say as Nicole drives up with everyone's lunch.

With sandwiches in hand, Nicole drives us back to our motorhome so we can take a quick break, eat and walk Leo. "It feels so good in here," Kait says as she walks inside. The AC is keeping the motorhome in the sixties, and Leo barely budges when we come inside. That is until he smells the sandwiches and jumps up to attention.

Stripping off my sweat-soaked shirt, I start unwrapping my sandwich and sit down on the couch. Leo follows me, never taking his eyes off my prize. "Okay, bud. I'll save a few pieces of chicken for you."

"So what do you think so far?" Kait asks.

"I wish it wasn't so hot, but I feel like we're getting through everything pretty quickly. Livorno said he thinks we should be done in a few hours. What do you think?"

"I don't know. In some ways I feel disingenuous, like when they ask me to talk about something I don't care about."

"Are you being honest when you talk about whatever it is?" I ask.

"Of course, but if I were shopping for a van, it's not something I would normally talk about."

"I think that's fine. I get that they need to be able to tell a story, and although it might not be something we're interested in, it might be for people who are watching. As long as we're honest about what we like and don't like, we're not being disingenuous at all."

"You're right. I'm just nervous about how we're going to be portrayed on the show."

"I think it will be fine," I tell Kait. "Why don't you finish your sandwich, and I'll take Leo for a walk around the park."

A few minutes later, Leo drags me back inside the motorhome. "Back so soon?" Kait asks.

"He peed, pooped then dragged me back here. I think he's much happier to be in the motorhome with the AC than walking around outside."

"I don't blame him, I wish I could stay here and relax all day," Kait says, leaning down to pet Leo. He rolls over as she scratches his belly and then we hear a knock at the door.

"Hey, guys, ready to head back?" Nicole asks when I open the door.

"Sure, give us a minute to grab our stuff," I respond.

As predicted, we're done a few hours later. Having learned a few lessons in the Era, the cameraman was able to get all of the shots they needed much more quickly in the Fuse and Travato. In each RV they had us talk about what we liked and didn't like. The Era has the best overall floorplan for us but a very cramped bathroom. The Fuse has much more room and a full bathroom, but in order to use the bed, a slide has to be put out. Considering we've been a few places where we couldn't put our slides out, this is a big negative for us. The Travato has a nice size bathroom for a van and we like the open layout up front, but the bed is very narrow. It's only forty-six inches wide which puts it between a twin and full size bed. I don't know if we could manage sleeping in a bed that small. Kait and I agree, between everything we saw, the Era is our favorite.

Walking back into our motorhome, it feels like a mansion after spending all day in those vans. Sitting on the couch and stretching out, I think that while I like the idea of going smaller, maybe it's not all it's cracked up to be. While we're not able to take this motorhome everywhere, I do like the extra space. The bathroom situation would be difficult and unless we got the Mercedes, we wouldn't be able to tow a car. Kait reminds me that we can always shower at the campground or get a membership to a national gym. If we wanted to keep the Jeep, we could drive separately which would give me some time alone to relax and listen to my podcasts. She makes some great points and we spend the rest of the evening discussing the pros and cons of going smaller.

Day two of filming goes even quicker than the first. When the crew showed up at 10, we were sitting outside in the cool morning air with Leo drinking our coffee. They weren't recording any audio inside the motorhome so we got to keep the AC on, and there was plenty of room for everyone to maneuver. The first set of shots were of me working and Kait standing over the stove making a meal. Leo rose to the occasion and instantly became the star of the show. Normally, when he does something cute or funny and we try to film it, he'll stop and walk away. We always tell people he's camera shy, but as soon as the cameras started rolling this morning, he went to work. Walking directly to the camera, he sat down and gave his best "husky face." The cameraman would move around the motorhome, calling Leo to come towards the camera and Leo obeyed every single time. Kait and I just had to laugh and shake our heads. At least he hams it up in front of the camera when it's for network television.

After about thirty minutes, the crew has us pack up the motorhome and hit the road. Kait jumps behind the wheel and their chase vehicle follows us onto the interstate with a camera man dangling out of the window. Meanwhile, a second cameraman was stationed in the motorhome getting shots of Kait driving.

By noon we're filming the close of the show where we talk about the three different RVs and which one we pick, which happens to be the Winnebago Era. That's followed by a quick drive in the Era with me behind the wheel. By 3:30 in the afternoon, we're done and home with Leo.

"That was a lot of fun, but I don't think I would want to do it again," Kait says.

"Neither would I, but it was a great learning experience. I have a lot of ideas on how we can improve the videos we're making using cutaway shots and a few other techniques I picked up. I was also talking to the sound guy about how we can improve the sound in our videos. He gave me a few suggestions of gear that's inexpensive but should work very well for our purposes."

"That's great," Kait says and sits next to me on the couch. "Where do you want to go next?"

BONUS CONTENT: While we were being filmed, we decided to grab some behind-the-scenes shots of our experience: https://youtu.be/1ZJr_9Ib5OE

19. SERVICE WORK

After shooting the TV show, we decided to spend an extra night at the campground to relax and get some work done. The last few days have been pretty hectic, and we both needed some time to just unwind.

It's after 10 in the morning, and I could have slept for another couple hours, but I had to use the bathroom and don't feel like crawling back into bed. "Now that you're awake would you mind putting the blinds up so we can get some natural light in here?" Kait asks from the couch as I come out of the bathroom.

"Sure," I say as I start working my way around to each of the windows. "What time did you get up this morning?"

"I don't know, maybe 7:30?"

The last shade to be put up is the large one on the front window. I press the button to raise the shade, and as it's coming up I see something I've been dreading. On our drive through Texas, we got a rock chip in the window and, despite the fact we had it repaired, there is now a crack from one side of the windshield to the other.

"Damnit! The front windshield is cracked."

How'd that happen?" Kait asks.

"My guess is that when we were leveling the coach yesterday after the drive for the TV show, the windshield cracked. The motorhome probably twisted just enough to put pressure on it."

"Do you think we should call Newmar and see what they say?" Kait asks.

"That's not a bad idea. I think this is covered by our insurance, but I don't think replacing a windshield this size is an easy task." The windshield is probably about five feet high and seven or eight feet wide, and my guess is that the process is quite more complicated than replacing a car's windshield.

A few phone calls later to our insurance company and Newmar, I've added this to the list of things Newmar is going to repair during our appointment on May 23rd. Their service rep told me that replacing a windshield is the one thing they absolutely recommend people have done at the factory. They've heard too many complaints from customers who have the repair done by third parties. The downside is that Newmar charges more than the company our insurance wants us to use, which means they'll only cover a portion of the repair.

"We're all set," I tell Kait. "Newmar said with the windshield and other warranty repairs, we should plan to spend the entire week there."

"It's a good thing they have an RV park on-site and we can stay in the motorhome while they're working on it," Kait says. "I do have some good news for you. I just ran our income report for March and we made $403."

"Wow, that's awesome, congratulations! We're getting close to covering our monthly payment on the motorhome. I can't wait for the day we can actually cover all our monthly expenses."

"One day. It's just good to see our income going up every month. Let's hope this continues."

Tuesday, May 24th, 2016

5:15 a.m. The alarm goes off for the second day in a row and we both force ourselves out of bed. I don't have time to make coffee, so I grab a packet of instant I have stored for emergencies like this. This really isn't an emergency, but the technicians will be taking our motorhome in forty-five minutes, so if I want coffee, instant is my best option.

"Did you grab everything you need?" Kait asks as she packs her backpack.

"I think so. I have my laptop, chargers and a packet of coffee. We left everything else in the Jeep. I'm going to get the shore power cord unplugged and then bring the slides in so the motorhome is ready to go when they get here."

At 6 a.m. sharp we hear a golf cart pull up followed by a knock on the door.

"Morning, Joe," Kevin, our assigned technician says when I open the door. "You guys ready?"

"Morning, Kevin. Pretty much. Kait's just grabbing her bags, and then you can take the motorhome. What time do you think we'll get it back today?"

"We're going to have to keep it overnight. We're replacing the windshield today, and it needs to set overnight so you won't have it back until tomorrow afternoon."

"No one said anything about needing to keep it overnight," I respond. "What are we supposed to do for the night? We don't have a reservation anywhere, we haven't packed anything, and we have our dog."

"I'm very sorry. Someone should have notified you. The front desk can give you the name of a couple hotels in the area you can stay at, and we can wait a few minutes for you to get your things."

"Kait," I say stepping back inside. "Kevin says they're going to keep the motorhome overnight, and we'll need to get a hotel."

"What? No one said anything about keeping the motorhome overnight."

"I know. I'm not happy about it, but let's get some stuff packed, and we can regroup in the waiting area."

When we made our appointment with Newmar to bring our motorhome to the factory for warranty work, we were told they had a first come, first served campground on site we could stay at. They'd take the motorhome each day around six in the morning, work on it and return it sometime in the afternoon, allowing us to stay in it each night. We were also told to expect to be there a week but that it would probably take less time.

Last Friday we pulled into the lot at Newmar and grabbed one of the last sites available at the campground. They're full hookup, so we were happy to have snagged one. Once we were settled, we spent the weekend touring the city of Nappanee, Indiana, and doing a final walk-through of the motorhome to make sure there weren't any new issues that needed to be addressed. Although we had already provided Newmar with a list of warranty issues, we were told we could continue to add to the list until we met with the service techs the first day of our appointment. We found a few more minor issues, and yesterday at six in the morning, we went through the list with Kevin and were told they should have everything done no later than Friday of this week.

We've learned through talking to other RVers and reading things online that all new RVs have issues that need to be worked out. Issues can range from a loose piece of moulding to a slide that isn't working. Having a one year warranty allows us to put the motorhome through its paces and work out any bugs. We did see some suggestions online that if we wanted to avoid having to work out the bugs, to look for a used unit that's a year or two old since the previous owner <u>may</u> have had all the bugs taken care of.

Leo is still passed out by the time we're ready to leave. We've learned that at this hour, there's no coaxing him out of bed. So what I end up doing is taking his leash and clipping it on him while he's in bed. Then at least he gets up and begrudgingly follows me outside to the Jeep and promptly goes back to sleep, not wanting to be bothered. Although it's been hot during the day, it's still quite cool in the mornings, so we can put the windows down for him while he sleeps. Once it gets warm, we take him on a long walk and then sit with him in the shade until our motorhome is back from service.

Walking into the waiting room, I head over to the hot water dispenser, pour the instant coffee into my mug and fill it with water. Apparently I didn't learn my lesson yesterday because as soon the coffee granules have dissolved, I take a sip, burning my tongue. Kait notices the look on my face and shakes her head at me.

"I'm worried we won't be able to find a hotel that allows dogs," Kait says as we sit down on a leather couch.

"Me too," I respond. "There aren't many places to stay around here but we can ask the receptionist if she can recommend a place. I'm sure this isn't the first time someone with a dog needed to get a room."

"If we can't find a place, I'm going to Walmart, buying a tent and camping in the parking lot with Leo," Kait states in a very strong tone.

Laughing, I take another sip of my coffee and ask, "Am I not invited?"

"You are. I'm just saying that's what Leo and I are doing. I know you don't like sleeping on the ground because of your back, so you can stay in a hotel and we'll sleep here."

When the office opens, we're given a couple options for hotels in the area that allow dogs. We call the first one on the list and, lucky for us, they have a few rooms available. When we arrive at the hotel, the room we've booked is pretty run down. We both assume they put people with dogs in these rooms and not the nicer ones. It makes sense, but it is one of the reasons we chose to travel in a motorhome and not stay in hotels along the way. We've been on the road for eight months, and this is the first night we will have been out of our "home."

Crawling into bed, Kait cuddles up with me and says, "I keep thinking about going smaller. This experience has reminded me of why I don't want a big RV."

"We're going to have problems with any RV, big or small."

"I know, but there are just so many more things to go wrong with bigger RVs. I don't want slides, hydraulic jacks and the giant front windshield."

"I'd love to get something without slides. Knock on wood, we haven't had a problem with ours, but I've met a few people in the waiting room who are here because they're having issues with theirs."

"Why don't we go check out some smaller RVs while we're here and see if we find anything we like," Kait says, rising up on her elbows so she can look me directly in the eye. "If we're going to stay on the road, I want to get something smaller."

"We're going to take a loss on the Newmar if we sell it. We're also a long way from covering our monthly expenses each month and only have so much left in savings. I don't think it makes financial sense for us to switch RVs right now."

"I know, but we're making more each month which is extending the amount of time we can spend on the road. I don't want to buy anything right away but I think we can start planning. I truly believe we can reach our goal of making enough to cover our expenses by the end of the year."

"It would be awesome if we could meet that goal. This month has been going really well for us but covering our expenses seems so far off, especially when we have to pay over $800 for a new windshield."

Kait seems to be lost in thought for a minute, then says, "I was just thinking. Why don't we evaluate the decision to move to a smaller RV at the end of the year? See what our financial situation is like and if we're still interested in going smaller."

"I think that's a great idea. I'm still game to check out some small RVs to see if we can find something we like. Maybe even check out a few small trailers we can tow with the Jeep?"

"Oh, that's a good idea!" Kait says with a huge smile, laying back down onto the bed. It's been a long, stressful day, and within a few minutes, she's asleep. I'm excited about the prospects of moving to a smaller RV, I just wonder if we'll really hit our goal of making enough money to cover our expenses by year's end. At our current burn rate and income, we could probably go another year with the savings we have left. It'll be hard to justify moving to something else if we aren't putting any money back in the bank by that point.

Sunday, June 12th, 2016

Three weeks after we arrived at the Newmar factory for warranty work, we're ready to go. Delays with some of the repairs and additional items we found kept us at the service center two weeks longer than we initially expected. I'm very grateful they were able to accommodate us and get everything taken care of. After the first week, as we were getting ready to leave, Kait suggested we wash the motorhome before getting on the road. While we were drying it, Kait found some issues with the paint. Luckily, Newmar was able to take us the following week to get everything dealt with so we got to spend some more time touring around Nappanee and the surrounding area.

This is Amish country, and most of the factory workers at Newmar are Amish, so we got accustomed to hearing the horse and buggies at five each morning arriving at work. I always found it interesting to see the juxtaposition of the Amish walking around the factory floor with iPads and building motorhomes, then at the end of the day, getting in their buggy to head home.

Speaking of the Amish, our biggest mistake while we were there was going to the Amish bakery, Rise'n Roll. It is a couple miles from Newmar and everyone told us we had to go and get some donuts. They had the best apple fritters I've ever had and my few extra pounds are a testament to that.

When I wasn't eating apple fritters, or they were sold out, we spent time going on a few factory tours of different motorhome companies. This area of Indiana, particularly Elkhart, is considered the RV capital of the world with more than eighty percent of global production based in the area. It was eye-opening to see how different manufacturing was from factory to factory, and we saw a distinct difference in quality between each one. We had the opportunity to drive a few small motorhomes and are beginning to get a feel for what we like and don't like in the small spaces. I definitely want something like a small Class C with a full bath and not the wet baths we keep seeing in Class B vans and Kait seems to prefer the vans and their smaller footprint.

I still have some lingering doubts that a small RV is going to work for us. Our Newmar Bay Star has over 4,000 pounds of carrying capacity. The small motorhomes and vans have anywhere from 400 to 1,000 pounds after you deduct the weight of us, Leo and a full tank of water. Even if we can get rid of a lot of stuff, that's not much carrying capacity for two people who plan to live in it full-time. We're going to have to do some real soul-searching to see if this is something we're sure we want to pursue.

TIP FROM THE ROAD: Since your rolling home experiences an earthquake every time it goes down the road, you'll experience issues ranging from small things that are nothing more than an annoyance, to major issues that keep you from making it to your next destination. Depending on the location and time of year, dealerships might be booked out months in advance so if you're stuck, consider calling a mobile tech who may be able to come to you that day. Also, try to learn to fix things yourself. Even if your RV is still under warranty, fixing the little things can save you a lot of time and hassle if you don't have to take it to a dealer to have it dealt with.

BONUS CONTENT: Here's a breakdown of all of our experiences getting service work done on our Newmar Bay Star: https://weretherussos.com/newmar-warranty-and-customer-service/

20. THE C WORD

Saturday, July 31st, 2016

"I can't believe we just spent seven days at the show," Kait says as we're pulling out of the parking lot on our last day of the Oshkosh Air Show. "It's been a lot of fun, but I'm ready for a break."

A week ago, we walked onto the busiest airfield in the world (well, busiest that week) for the EAA AirVenture Oshkosh show, better known simply as the Oshkosh Air Show. With over 10,000 aircraft, the Oshkosh Air Show has been on my bucket list since I first heard of it as a child. I've always been a huge WWII aircraft buff and lived my dream when I got to stand fifty feet from a P51 Mustang and F4U Corsair as they started their engines and taxied away to fly overhead with a variety of other aircraft from the era. Putting my hand on a P40 Warhawk sent shivers down my spine. Seven days later, I can honestly say that I need a break from the old warbirds. Oshkosh was an amazing experience, but I'm happy it's over (Video of our first day at EAA: https://youtu.be/LTdCJNsAg5I).

"Do you think Leo will be up on the dash when we get back?" I ask.

Since dogs aren't allowed at the air show, Leo has been hanging out in the motorhome while we've been gone. The weather has been hot and humid, so he's been happy to stay back and bask in the ice cold AC. The first day we got back to the motorhome, he was asleep with his head poking out from under the front shade. The next day we left the shade up, and, once again, when we got home he was up on the dash, lying against the window, sound asleep.

"I'd be more surprised if he wasn't," Kait replies. "That's become his new favorite spot. I think he likes to watch everything go by. Plus, he knows he's not allowed up there, so I think he does it just to annoy us."

"Sounds about right. Gotta love huskies," I respond.

As expected, when we pull up, Leo is passed out on the dash and acknowledges our arrival by giving us a dirty look for bothering him before jumping down. Walking inside the motorhome, I turn the AC up to seventy-two. It's freezing inside and one of the reasons Leo is hesitant to go out for a bathroom break.

As I sit down on the couch, my phone starts ringing.

"Hey, Mom, what's up?" I ask, putting her on speaker.

"Hey, Joe," she says in a nervous tone. "I have some news I want to share with you and Kait."

From her tone, I know it isn't good and I get a bad feeling in the pit of my stomach. "Kait's here with me, and I have you on speaker. Go ahead."

"Okay. Do you remember when I had a scan done of my lungs last year and they found some nodes?"

"I remember."

"Well, one of the nodes has grown and my doctor is concerned it might be cancer. He wants to go in, remove the node and check it for cancer. If it's cancerous, he's going to remove the area of my lung around the node."

When my mother was growing up, there were ads that promoted smoking as being healthy and recommended by doctors. During college, cigarette companies would hand out free packs to the students and she, like many of her peers, started smoking. Growing up, I remember my parents smoking multiple packs per day. My sister and I hated the smoke and would beg them to quit. They tried at times, but my mother had a serious addiction and would become violently ill every time she stopped. As I was getting into my early teens, children and teachers at school would ask me if I smoked. My clothes and books smelled like cigarettes. Something about that finally clicked and my mom got medical help to quit and was finally able to kick the habit. However, the damage had been done.

"When's your surgery?" I ask.

"The second week of September. I wasn't going to tell you and your sister because I didn't want you to worry. This should just be a minor procedure."

"You didn't want us to worry? Mom, lung surgery isn't minor, and what if something happens? I want to be there, and you're going to need help recovering. I don't think you'll just be able to walk out of the hospital and go back to work the following Monday."

"That's why I didn't want to tell you. I know you and Kait are planning to go to that big RV show in Pennsylvania, and I don't want you to change your plans. It's really not necessary for you to be here."

"Mom, I'm coming home. What are you going to do about Jason's wedding at the end of August?"

"I'm still going; he's my God child. That's why I'm waiting until September to have my surgery. You and Kait are going too, right? I hope so, because your cousin is really looking forward to meeting Kait."

"We were planning on it, and then we were going to head to Pennsylvania for the RV show. I guess now we'll just book it to Los Angeles after the wedding for your surgery," I say looking over at Kait. She's nodding her head in confirmation. I know she wants to be there as much as I do. It will be a long drive cross country, but my mother has a habit of understating how serious something like this can be, and I want to be there to help and support her.

"Ah, honey," my mom says with a deep sadness. "I don't want you to have to do that on my account. I'll be fine; don't worry about me."

"Mom, if I don't come home, I'll be a nervous wreck! Plus," I say with a joking tone, "if I don't come home, I'll never hear the end of how you were in surgery for lung cancer and your own son didn't even come home to be there. Just like that time when you were admitted to the ER for that infection and Dad called you to ask what was for dinner."

My mom starts laughing and I can tell she feels relieved. I can only imagine how this has been weighing on her, and I know she'd never ask me to come home, but there's nothing in the world she wants more than my sister and me to be there when they wheel her into the operating room.

"Let's just make sure to have a lot of fun at the wedding in case I don't make it through surgery," she says in a very lighthearted tone.

"Can't wait," I say. "Love you, Mom."

As I put my phone down, Kait wraps me in her arms as I break into tears. I lost my father three years ago and I'm not ready to lose my mother. That said, I'm very thankful for the fact that this lifestyle allows us to change our plans at a moment's notice to go be with my mother. I don't have to worry about checking in with work and taking time off. Instead, I can focus on being there for my mom and spending as much time as needed.

Gaining my composure, I lean back and ask, "So are you good with driving to L.A.?"

"Of course, honey. We're not going to have much time after the wedding to drive out there, but if we do some long driving days, we should make it back in time for you to have a few days to spend with your mom before the surgery."

"That'd be nice. It's too bad we're going to miss the Hershey RV show in Pennsylvania. I was really looking forward to checking out the smaller RVs. Hymer is supposed to be there with the new Aktiv, and I remember how much we liked the Grand Canyon prototype at the Tampa show."

Earlier this week, we hit 4,000 subscribers on our YouTube channel and income from our website and channel has been growing twenty-five percent month over month. The final numbers aren't in yet but it looks like we made almost $1,300 in July, which covers half of our expenses. If this rate of growth continues, we should have no problem hitting our goal by the end of the year.

Seeing this trend, we decided that we'd start seriously looking at smaller RVs. Hershey is one of the largest shows in the country, so we planned to use the show as a way to see everything at once and hopefully make up our minds as to what we want.

"There will be other shows," Kait says, putting her hand on my leg. She has a contemplative look on her face as she picks up her phone and starts typing something into the browser. A minute later, she looks up from the screen, smiling. "The California RV show is in early October, and Hymer is going to be there as well. That will give us time to spend with your mom after her surgery, and we can check out all the small RVs there."

"That works out well," I say. "I just hope everything goes well with my mom's surgery."

"It will."

21. THEY CALLED SECURITY

I haven't seen my cousin Jason since his father's funeral almost ten years ago. When I was kid, Jason came to live with us for a year while he was going to school in California. Looking back, that year was one of the best memories I had as a child, and Jason has always had a special place with me. That's why when we were invited to his wedding, I told Kait I'd like to make the detour to Ohio so we could attend.

When we learned about the wedding, we had planned on being somewhere on the East Coast. If we flew out for the wedding, we'd have to board Leo, which is something we didn't want to do, so we decided to change our plans and stay in the Midwest until the wedding. That's how we ended up going to the Oshkosh Air Show. It's a good thing too, because if we'd stuck to our original plan, we would have had a much longer drive to Los Angeles for my mother's surgery.

"What's the date of Jason's wedding?" Kait asks, opening the large paper map we have of the United States and setting it on the dinette table.

"August 27th."

"And your mom's surgery is on September 8th, right? That gives us twelve days to get from the wedding to California."

Kait lays her iPhone on the map and begins typing. A minute later she looks up and says, "It's about 2,400 miles from the wedding in Ohio to your mom's house. If we average 500 miles a day, that should give you almost a week with her before the surgery. Would that work?"

"Sure," I respond.

"What's wrong?"

"I'm worried because of what happened with my dad. Every time I think about the surgery, I feel sick to my stomach."

When my dad was diagnosed with lung cancer, the doctors said they had found it early and just needed to do targeted radiation on it. Quick in and out procedure, no cutting him open and he'd be fine. They got the cancer, but shortly after he had that treatment, he started going downhill. It started with his breathing and then cascaded to everything else. He was gone less than a year later. I sometimes wonder if he'd still be here if he'd never had that procedure done and I'm scared something similar will happen with my mom.

Kait gets up from the dinette and sits down next to me, wrapping me in her arms. "I know it's scary, but your mom is tough. She's also a lot younger and healthier than your dad was. If anyone is going to make it through something like this, it's going to be her."

"I know you're right," I say, wiping a tear off my cheek.

Looking back down at the map, I consider asking my mom if she'd like to drive with us back to Los Angeles. After a moment however, I realize with the miles we're planning on driving, there wouldn't be much time to see anything. Plus we're probably going to end up sleeping at rest areas or parking lots and I don't think my mom would enjoy that too much. "So where do we head first after the wedding?" I ask.

Friday, August 26th, 2016

We found a campground a couple miles from Jason's home in Ohio. The place is an RV and water park combo.

When we pulled in yesterday, the water park was packed with people. It's been in the nineties and very humid so we weren't surprised, even though it was midday on a Thursday. After checking in, we spent the day exploring the area and then went over to Jason's house to see everyone.

Jason and his fiancé decided to have a small, informal wedding and reception in their backyard. We were told to dress like we were going to a nice pool party. I was relieved to hear that because "dressed up" these days means a pair of jeans and a button-down shirt. If it's "fancy," I might leave the flip-flops behind and wear shoes.

With the heat and humidity, Leo hasn't been too eager to go outside. We've been taking him on long walks in the morning and at night when it's a bit cooler, but most of the time he just wants to enjoy the AC. Even when we went over to Jason's house, Leo had full run of their yard but wanted to stay inside where it was cool. We got lucky with our spot at the campground because the motorhome is shaded for most of the day, and since we're plugged into shore power, we can run the AC non-stop.

Looking down at Leo, Kait says, "Bubs, it's cold in here. What's the AC set to?"

"Sixty-eight," I respond for Leo.

Shaking her head, Kait asks, "Should we bring Leo with us again to Jason's house?"

"Let's leave him here. I think he's going to be much happier in the motorhome than outside. Plus we're just going for some pizza and shouldn't be gone too long. I'll take him for a walk now so he's a bit worn out. Should we turn the AC down anymore?"

"I don't want to be freezing when we get home. Let's leave it where it is."

"Okay, but let's put the front shade up so he can people watch while we're gone."

A few hours later we head home from dinner. When we get back to the RV park, the place is packed. Most of the seasonal sites are full with people partying. Everyone seems to have a BBQ set up, the alcohol is flowing, and one campsite seems to have turned into a nightclub of sorts.

As we get closer to our site, I notice a golf cart and two security officers standing in front of our neighbor's RV, talking to them.

"What do you think is going on?" Kait asks as I park the Jeep.

"I have no idea."

Stepping out of the Jeep, one of the officers turns and walks over to me and asks, "Is this your site?"

"Yes. Is something wrong?"

"Your neighbors filed a complaint that you left your dog in your motorhome without AC. They said some of the other neighbors were concerned as well since they could see your dog sitting in the front window."

I look over to see the neighbors staring at us and feel my blood pressure rise. "Are you serious? You can hear the AC running right now, and our dog looks fine," I say, pointing to Leo who is sound asleep on the dash of the motorhome, barely able to contain the anger in my voice.

"I understand, sir, but we had to check it out since they called us. We could tell when we drove up that your dog was fine. No need to get upset."

"Sorry. I'm not upset at you, just the situation."

"No problem. I'd suggest leaving the front shade down next time you go out. Have a good night," the officer says. He and his partner say something to our neighbors who don't look happy and then drive off in their golf cart.

Kait is livid when she steps inside. "I could understand their concern if we were boondocking and left the motorhome out in the sun, but we're parked in the shade under a huge tree, the sun is almost down and we're plugged into shore power. You can HEAR the AC running from outside."

"I know," I say, putting a hand on her shoulder. "We've never had an issue before, so I just say if we have to leave Leo while we're here, we put the front shade down. I know he loves to watch everyone, but he's going to have to take a few days off."

Before we hit the road, one of the things we were most concerned about was leaving our dogs in the motorhome while we were gone. We'd heard stories of power going out at RV parks or AC units failing while owners were away. However, now that we've been on the road for almost a year, we've realized that a motorhome doesn't heat up the same way a car does. The motorhome has much more insulation than a car and, if all the shades are down, very little sunlight comes in. Most of the time, we've found that if we leave a few windows open and run the exhaust fans, it will stay cooler in the motorhome than outside. Our rule of thumb has been that if we're not comfortable, he isn't. If we have to run the AC and leave Leo, we try not to leave him for more than a couple hours. That way, even if something does go wrong with the AC, it would still be cool inside by the time we got back.

The next morning Kait wakes up early to take Leo out. It's already hot but Leo's excited to stretch his legs. When they get back Kait's anger from the previous night has returned. "So Leo and I had an off-leash dog come after us when we went on our walk. Want to guess whose dog it was?"

"I have no idea, whose?"

"Our neighbor's. The same ones who called security on us. They also left their dogs outside in the sun. Maybe I should call security."

"Don't. Let's just leave it alone. We're going to be at the wedding today and don't need any other trouble from them while we're gone," I tell Kait.

The next morning as I'm getting dressed, Kait starts grabbing the tripod and our camera gear. When I ask what she's doing, she tells me that she wants to make a video telling people what happened. The reasoning is that since we get a lot of questions from people about what it's like to RV with a dog, we should show the bad along with the good. All of the videos we've done so far with Leo show us having fun and taking him places, but not the challenges. Plus, she wants to vent to someone (or something) besides me.

We take our gear well away from our neighbors, set up the camera and start talking about our experience. We ramble on for a while but after it's all over, we both feel much better and head back to the motorhome. One realization we both had as we were talking to the camera is that this experience is one reason why we don't like staying at RV parks. When you're boondocking, you typically don't have neighbors and if you do, you rarely see them. Shortly after we get back, I have the footage cut down and we decide to upload it right away to YouTube.

"We'd better get ready for the wedding," I tell Kait.

"I know, but now I'm nervous about leaving Leo while we're at the wedding. I couldn't sleep last night because I was reading a few articles about people breaking windows to rescue dogs from cars. I'm worried someone is going to break in and take Leo."

"He'll be fine, plus I'm happy to drive home to check on him during the wedding and take him for walks. My cousin's place is only a few minutes away, so it won't take long to drive over and check on him." My solution seemed to calm Kait down, and after a small breakfast and coffee, we started getting ready for the wedding.

The wedding went off without a hitch, and everyone had a great time. At different times during the day, I took a quick drive back to the campground with my nephew to check on things and walk Leo. My nephew loved coming over to see Leo and our "house." He was fascinated with the motorhome and couldn't believe that we actually lived in it. He's also an avid follower of our videos on YouTube, so he was excited to finally see it all in person.

Kait and I are both a bit apprehensive as we drive home after the wedding wondering if security will be there again or worse, but when we pull up to our camper and open the door, Leo is happily asleep on the couch.

The next morning over coffee, I open my laptop and start checking comments on the video we posted about our neighbors calling security. The video has gotten quite a few views as well as a lot of comments. As I scroll through them, I see a wide variety of opinions from people who understand why we're upset and other's getting downright angry at us. We're also getting a lot of helpful comments from people who are making suggestions like sticking a note in the window with our phone number or putting a thermometer in the window so people can see how cool it is inside.

While we appreciate all of the positive and helpful comments, it's hard reading all of the negative. We understand where some people are coming from, but, at the same time many are being nasty, calling us names and going so far as to threaten to break a window and take Leo if they ever see us on the road. It's a reminder that since we share our lives online, people are going to share their opinions about it.

BONUS CONTENT: Although we tried to help everyone get things ready for the wedding, there were just too many cooks in the kitchen so we were told to go off and do something else. Well, that's just what we did and spent a couple days exploring Canton, Ohio. Check out these 10 Fun Things to Do in Canton: https://weretherussos.com/things-to-do-in-canton-ohio/

22. GOING BACK TO CALI

Monday, August 29th, 2016

We pull out of the RV park early and get on the road. Our first stop is a friend's house outside of Indianapolis, Indiana. He's a former college friend that I haven't seen since graduation. While we were at the Newmar factory getting work done, we got an email from him saying that he watched some of our videos on YouTube and, not only did he find them helpful and inspiring, but he recognized me! He had retired early and was looking to travel in an RV and during his research, found our videos. We started emailing back and forth, and made plans to stop in and catch up.

We had planned to put in more miles, but I was excited to see Todd again, and Kait really wanted to meet him after some of the stories I had told her. We also saw that it was only going to get down into the high eighties in the evening so we accepted Todd's offer to sleep in one of his guest rooms. Leo was invited too.

The three of us spent the night catching up and it was like I had just seen Todd yesterday. We got right back into our old routine of ribbing each other, and Kait had a great time laughing at our expense. The next morning as we were saying our goodbyes, Todd handed us a large paper bag. He had snuck out early and picked up some goodies from a local bakery. Inside, we found a huge glazed cinnamon bun and a fresh loaf of bacon bread. Thanking him for the pounds we were about to gain, we waved goodbye and headed toward Interstate 70.

Our goal for the day was 500 miles, which would take us to Kanas City, Kansas. We chose this route over heading towards Oklahoma City because Kait told me about an amazing BBQ joint in KC for pulled pork sandwiches. We figured having some great food along the way would make up for having to stay on the interstate.

"I was just checking the map, and we're going to drive through St. Louis," Kait said once we were about an hour outside of Indy. "And you know what St. Louis is known for, don't you?"

"Ribs?"

"Exactly. I was just reading about one of the best spots in the city. Do you want to stop and get a slab?"

"Is that a rhetorical question? Of course, but where are we going to park the motorhome and Jeep?" I asked.

"I have no idea. I read there is street parking. Worst case we either find a lot to park in or you drop me off, and I'll get the ribs to go while you drive around."

Two hours later, we got off the interstate and followed the GPS's instructions to Bogart's Smokehouse. The closer we got, the more residential the area became. About a quarter-mile away on Lafayette Street, I saw the sign for the restaurant in the distance and a long stretch of empty street parking. I pulled the motorhome and Jeep over, parking as close to the curb as possible. I made sure to stop just before a driveway so that no one could park in front of us and block us in.

Since there was outdoor seating, we brought Leo, and I sat outside with him while Kait ordered. "What'd you get?" I asked when she came back out with a number.

"Uh, everything. I got a slab of ribs and small portions of the brisket, pulled pork and burnt ends along with pit beans, pickles and deviled egg salad."

"After our breakfast this morning, I may need to fast for a week!"

The BBQ was amazing. The ribs were the best we'd ever had. They were so tender the meat melted in our mouths and the slightly smoky, sweet flavor was perfect. No sauce needed. The pit beans were almost as good. They were cooked for 12 hours under the brisket to catch all of the drippings. This is a spot we will definitely plan to come back to.

After lunch, Kait asked to take the second leg of the trip, and shortly after we got back onto Interstate 70, a massive thunderstorm rolled in. The rain and wind was so strong, it was almost impossible to keep the motorhome between the lines, so Kait pulled off the interstate so I could drive. As luck would have it, as soon as I got back on the interstate, the storm had passed.

"There is a Walmart right across the street from the BBQ place, and it looks like they allow overnight parking," Kait said as we got close to Kansas City.

"That's convenient. We can park there, walk over, have dinner and then relax in the motorhome."

The Walmart turned out to be one of the smaller neighborhood stores. Although the parking lot was small, we still managed to find an area where we could park. After taking Leo for a walk, we went across the street to get our BBQ. We decided to get it to go since the restaurant was so busy and it's more comfortable for us to just eat at home.

"This isn't nearly as good as I remember," Kait said back in the motorhome after taking her first bite of the pulled pork sandwich.

"I'm not impressed," I told her. Along with my sandwich, I also got a few ribs to try. While we were standing in line, a local tried to convince me that this place had far better ribs than Bogart's. "I'm sorry to say, but the ribs and pulled pork at this place are a far cry from what we had in St. Louis. I should never have listened to that guy."

"Well, you didn't know, and they could have been amazing," Kait said. "By the way, with all of the eating out we're doing and the gas to go cross country, we're going to blow our monthly budget."

"I figured, but at least when we're at my mom's house we won't have too many added expenses to worry about."

We finished eating by eight and decided to get back on the road. I wasn't ready to call it a night and figured I could keep driving until I was tired. An hour later, the day finally caught up with me and I pulled into a rest area off Interstate 35 in Pomona, Kansas. All of the truck spots were taken, so I parked in a large open area toward the end of the lot, out of the way of the trucks. It hadn't cooled off much, but even with the warm weather, we were both asleep soon after we stopped.

The next two days on the road are uneventful as we head to Flagstaff. As much as I would like to get to Los Angeles and see my mom, we decided that a little downtime to decompress from the last few grueling days on the road was needed. We've come a long way from the white knuckle moments we had in the beginning and have no problem driving on narrow lanes in a construction zone now, but it's still exhausting after a long day in the saddle. It's great that Kait is willing to switch off driving with me, especially if I'm not feeling 100%. When we pull into an RV park and Kait's behind the wheel, we always have men tell us they wish their wives drove for that very reason.

When we arrived in Flagstaff, we headed back out to our dispersed camping spot in the national forest and spent three days relaxing and working in the cool, crisp mountain air.

Sunday, September 4th, 2016

At 5 p.m., we pull up to my mother's house in Los Angeles. It's strange to think that almost a year ago, we drove away from this very spot. When we left, this was going to be a one-year adventure with our dogs which has evolved into a nomadic lifestyle where we're living our dream and working for ourselves. So much has changed with us in the last twelve months.

It is in the nineties and a stark contrast to the forty degree weather we woke up to in Flagstaff this morning. My mother is overjoyed to see us, and we're already making plans on how we'll spend the next few days with her before the surgery. She's also excited to have a dog back in the house. Her yellow lab, Tucker, passed away about the same time Duke did, and she's been missing having a dog to love up on, so Leo gets a bigger hug than I did when we walked in the house. At least my mom had a cup of fresh coffee for me.

Looking back over the past week, we drove about 2,400 miles, averaging seven miles per gallon. Kait made the observation that it would have been less expensive for us to fly out to California than drive. However, there is something to be

TALES FROM THE OPEN ROAD

said about having your home with you at all times. It's comforting to be able to sleep in your own bed and not worry about leaving something behind. If the weather changes, you can easily change your clothes and be comfortable. Plus, if we had flown, we would have had to have boarded Leo and stored the RV. So while it would have been less expensive to fly, we much prefer to take our home wherever the journey leads.

Over a cup of coffee, my mom explains what the surgery will entail. She plays off the doctor's warning that she could be in the hospital for a week or more and should expect a few months to fully recover. My aunt lives with my mother, but I don't want to burden her with having to take care of my mom the entire time she is in recovery. It looks like we might be back in Los Angeles for a lot longer than we anticipated.

23. SURGERY

Thursday, September 8th, 2016

Surgery was scheduled for nine this morning. When we arrived at the hospital, my sister was there to meet us and we all got to spend some time together before my mother had to get prepped. That was six hours ago. The plan was that the doctor would go in and remove the node. Based on the results from pathology, her doctor would either remove the cancerous tissue around the node or close her up because the node was benign. The latter was only supposed to take an hour.

"I guess it must be cancer," I say to my sister, who's sitting across from me in the waiting area of the hospital.

"We don't know that. It might just be taking longer than expected."

"Five hours longer? I don't think so. I'm going to go check the monitor again to see if she's still in surgery."

The hospital has monitors in the waiting room to provide updates for waiting friends and family. My sister, aunt and I have been going back and forth every half hour to check on my mother's status. Each patient is assigned a code, and when I reach the monitors, I start searching for my mother's. It takes me a few minutes to realize the reason I don't see it is because her code has moved to the top of the screen and shows her status as, "Post Op." A sense of relief washes over me and I report back to my sister and aunt.

"You look pretty good," I say as we walk into my mother's room almost two hours later. "How do you feel?"

"I'm feeling pretty good. A bit groggy but I'm not in any pain," she says with a smile and an "I told you so" look.

"Well, take it easy. Your doctor said that they gave you a nerve block, so that's probably why you're not in pain. He told us that he had to remove ten percent of your left lung. The node came back cancerous, so he removed it along with some of the tissue surrounding it, which they'll be testing as well."

"He told me the same thing a few minutes before you got up here," my mom says. "When I asked him how long I'd have to stay here, he said until I could get up and walk around without help. So help me up. I want to do some walking. I intend to get out of this place as quickly as possible.

"Mom, I don't think that's a good idea," my sister says with a look of concern on her face. "You should rest a bit before you try and get up. The doctor told us you'll probably be here for at least four days before you can go home."

Turning towards my sister, she says, "I feel fine, and the doctor said I could get up and start walking whenever I felt up to it. Now, Joe, come over here and help me with all of these wires."

Arguing with my mother at this point is pointless. She hates hospitals and she's determined not to spend a minute longer here than she has to. "Hold on a minute, mom," I say looking over all the equipment she's hooked into. "I need to find your nurse and find out how we can take all of this apart so you can walk."

At the nurses' station, I have to repeat my request multiple times. Apparently my mother is the first person to demand that she be allowed to walk shortly after having a portion of her lung removed. "Let me call the doctor and make sure he's comfortable with letting her get out of bed so soon," the nurse says.

Ten minutes later, the nurse walks into my mother's room and says, "I spoke to your doctor and he said that you can get up and take a short walk whenever you feel ready."

"I'd like to get up now. Can you unhook me from these so I can take a walk?" My mom asks, holding up wires and the tube to the IV.

"We can't unhook you, but the monitor and IV will work off battery," the nurse says. "All we need to do is unplug it from the wall. I can walk with you to the nurses' station and back to make sure you don't fall."

"No, I want to walk around the floor. My son can hold me up and will walk with me. Come on, Joe; let's go."

Surprisingly the nurse doesn't argue and begins unhooking the machine from the wall. I look over at my sister and see her shaking her head with a smile. We know there is no arguing with my mother, so I put one arm out so she can hold onto it and use the other to grab the stand the IV and monitor are attached to.

"How many steps have we done?" My mom asks once we've gone past the nurses station for the fifteenth time.

Pulling out my phone, I open the Health app and giggle. "Minus what I did earlier today, 4,000. You ready to take a break?"

"I think so. I'm getting a bit tired and would like to sit down for a while," she responds with a triumphant smile.

Thirty minutes later, she tells me she's ready to go again so we rack up another few thousand steps. It seems like the day is catching up with her so she decides to rest and I tell her I'll be back in the morning. I've had a few sleepless nights from all the stress, but seeing my mom walk almost three miles around the hospital has made all that go away. When I get back to the motorhome, Kait and Leo are waiting for me with a hot dinner. She decided to stay behind and take care of Leo since we had no idea how long we'd be gone. Shortly after dinner, I crawl in bed and am asleep as soon as my head hits the pillow.

I wake to the sound of my phone buzzing. The sun is up and Kait is sitting in bed. Picking my phone up, I see a text from my mom.

"Don't worry about coming to the hospital today. Doctor released me this morning and your sister is coming to pick me up. I've been making the nurses take me for walks and I think they got tired of trying to stop me and decided to send me home. See you and Kait in a few hours. Love mom."

"What's so funny?" Kait asks looking over at me.

"It's my mom. They're kicking her out of the hospital because they can't keep up with her."

"Your mother is amazing," Kait says with a laugh.

Over the next few weeks, Kait and I keep the motorhome parked in front of my mom's house. Although my mom has a guest bedroom in the house for us, we prefer to sleep in our own bed. We do take her up on the offer to use the shower and bathroom so we don't have to worry about our tanks.

My mother is a bit slow to recover from the surgery because she continually pushes herself more than she should. She has me take her to the beach so we can walk five to six miles and then the next day she'll struggle to walk around the house. Of course, I'm her son, so she doesn't listen when I tell her to pace herself. It's only when the doctor echoes my statement that she decides to heed the advice. Speaking of her doctor, she got an all clear from him. Although the node was cancerous, the tissue he removed from around the node is cancer-free, which was a huge relief for all of us. (Here's a video I made a week after my mother's surgery...and yes, we were out for a long walk: https://youtu.be/rn-ObKDcsmU)

Leading up to my father passing away three years ago, my family and I had to juggle who would take him to the doctor, be there with him when he was in the hospital and care for him at home. We all worked full-time and none of us were able to be there 100% of the time. Looking back on this whole situation, I'm grateful that Kait and I now live this lifestyle and work for ourselves. We were able to drive to California, take all the time we needed with my mother and not have to worry about going into the office or asking for time off. This epitomizes the freedom and flexibility we now have in our lives which allows us to experience things in a new way. It's great getting to travel and see the country, but the ability to be there for our family and friends is priceless.

24. CALIFORNIA RV SHOW

Thursday, October 6th, 2016

Almost a month after my mother's surgery, she's close to being back to her normal self and we said goodbye a few days ago. As we were saying our goodbyes and walking out to the motorhome, I noticed chalk marks around the front tire. Apparently, someone in the neighborhood had called the police about our motorhome being parked on the street. Los Angeles only allows a vehicle to be parked on a street for a few days before it has to be moved, but I was hoping that, being parked in front of my mom's house, we'd be okay. Kait made the comment that if we had a smaller RV, we could just park in her driveway and not worry about it.

Our first stop was one of our favorite camping spots right along the beach, Rincon Parkway. After spending a few days there to recharge, we got on the road this morning to head to the California RV Show in Pomona. These last few days have been a trip down memory lane. Rincon Parkway was the first place we ever camped in our motorhome and Pomona was the first RV show we ever went to. We were still working at the time, and it brings back fond memories of how excited we were to take those first steps towards this life.

"When we were at this show in 2014, we told ourselves we were only considering diesel pushers that were thirty-eight feet or longer," I say to Kait as we head east down the 210 freeway.

"Yep, and now we're looking at camper vans. We've come a long way. When's our meeting with Susan from Hymer?"

After meeting the Hymer folks in Tampa, we've kept in touch through email. Susan joined the team a few months ago and we've been emailing back and forth ever since. When we told her we were going to be at this show, she asked if we could set up a time to meet and discuss how we could work together. Neither Kait nor I have any idea what she's looking to do, but we're excited to see the Hymer again.

"It's on your birthday," I respond with a smile.

"Well, I hope you didn't get me anything. If we're going to downsize to a van, we're going to have to get rid of a lot more stuff."

There is a campground right next to the RV show but we figured it would be pretty crazy over there and opted to camp about ten miles away at Prado Regional Park which has full hook ups and is well away from the crowds. We had thought about trying to find a place we could boondock but with the temperatures pushing ninety each day, we'll need to run the AC for Leo, which means the electric hook-up is going to be essential.

After getting set up we head over to Costco, leaving Leo in the motorhome. One nice thing about our lifestyle is that we can go shopping while most people are at work so the stores are never too busy. We stock up on a few staples and grab plenty of samples while we cruise through the warehouse.

As I am emptying our cart onto the conveyor at the checkout stand, I hear, "Hey Russos!" Looking up, a man in his mid-forties is looking back at me with a huge smile. "I watch your videos. What are you guys doing in this area?"

"We're here for the RV show," I say with a big smile, extending my hand. "I'm Joe."

He shakes it and says, "I know."

"Yes, but I don't know who you are," I respond with a smile.

"Oh, I'm sorry. My name's Dan. I just feel like I know you guys from all your videos."

"Hey, Dan, nice to meet you. This is Kait." Kait shakes his hand and finishes putting all of our items onto the conveyor.

"It's so nice to meet you two. I was shocked when I turned around and saw you guys," Dan says as he finishes paying. "I need to get going, but enjoy the show and keep making those videos!"

Pushing our full shopping cart out to the Jeep, I look over at Kait and ask, "What are the chances that someone would recognize us at Costco?"

"Considering we've got around 7,000 subscribers and almost a million views, I'm not too surprised. It was pretty cool getting to meet Dan. I wonder if anyone will recognize us at the show?"

"I think we might get a few people who do," I say, opening the door to the Jeep.

Friday, October 7th, 2016

This is the first day of the show. While most RV shows run between three to five days, the California show goes for ten. Since we'll stay for most of it, our plan is to head to the show today since it won't be as crowded as this weekend, get a lay of the land and film a quick video about what we see. We're also going to take Leo with us. While he dislikes the humidity, he loves the hot, dry weather of southern California.

By the time we get to the show, there is a small crowd. Passing rows of luxury Class A motorhomes, we don't even glance over. We're on a mission. When we first came to this show, Kait and I were overwhelmed. We didn't have a game plan and no idea of what we were looking for. We spent most of our time looking at half-million dollar motorhomes we couldn't afford, rather than focusing on what fit our budget. This time, however, we sat down and put together a list of must haves. We decided we want something small enough to fit into a parking spot and have a comfortable place to sleep and work. Before coming to the show, we made a video entitled, "RV Show Survival Guide," to help people learn from our mistakes.

"Oh, is that Sportsmobile?" Kait asks, pointing to a very mean looking Ford Econoline van that is raised high off the ground with big tires, armored bumpers and their signature pop top roof.

"Yep, that's Sportsmobile. I'd really like to take a look at that Ford."

Sportsmobile has quite the display. The Ford we see is their new concept vehicle with a sticker price just over $150,000. According to the president of the company, this thing will pretty much go anywhere, and people even take them rock climbing. They also have a few of their Mercedes Sprinter van conversions, similar to what we saw at the Tampa RV show. They're all 4x4 models and have many of the same accessories bolted to them that the Ford does, with a very similar price tag. Kait and I are in awe. We learn that

Sportsmobile custom builds vans for their customers. Don't like the layout or certain features? No problem. Tell them what you do want and they'll build it, within reason.

"Those things were awesome but WAY out of our price range," I say to Kait with a huge grin on my face as we walk away from their booth.

"We should see if we can find any used," she suggests. "Where to next?"

"Let's head over to Winnebago. I really like the Era we saw when we shot the TV show and I'd like to check out the Travato again."

Kait and I take turns touring the Era while the other one hangs with Leo in the shade. The Era is just as nice as we remember, and they seem to have taken a cue from Sportsmobile, as this one is on the 4x4 Mercedes chassis. Although it's very well appointed inside, our biggest concern with it is the layout. The rear couch transforms into a bed, which means we'd have to make the bed every night or not use our "living room." While it might not bother people who use this to camp for a long weekend, living in it full-time might prove otherwise.

"This one is almost $140,000," Kait says as we step out of the Era. "That's way out of our budget too, plus I don't think the bedroom slash living room is going to work for us."

"Neither do I. Most of the vans on the Mercedes chassis are going to be about $30,000 more than the ones on the Ram ProMaster chassis."

I explain that the biggest difference between the two is the Mercedes is diesel while the Ram is gas. There are pluses and minuses to each. The Mercedes is going to get better fuel mileage, but diesel fuel is more expensive in many places and you'd have to drive a lot to make up the difference in price between this and the Ram. The maintenance on the Mercedes is also going to be more expensive, and there are fewer Mercedes dealerships than Ram.

"What chassis is the Travato on?" Kait asks.

"It's on the Ram. Let's go check out the 59K. If I remember correctly, the one we looked at on Big Time RV was the 59G with that small bed in the back."

The layout of the Travato is completely different from the Era. Directly across from the big sliding door along the passenger side is a small kitchen area. The driver and passenger seats turn around to make a kind of living room area. There are small pull-out tables for each seat. Past the kitchen there are two twin beds on either side of the van. My favorite feature, however, is that they've taken the rear section of the van and turned it into a bathroom. This seems like one of the largest bathrooms we've seen in a van, and the neat feature is that you can use it with the rear doors open. If you're out in the middle of the woods, you can shower or use the toilet with the doors open to nature.

With everything we've seen so far, the Sportsmobiles and Travato with the rear bath are our favorites. If it weren't for the high price tag, Sportsmobile would be at the top of the list, but it's just beyond our budget. We love the features, four-wheel-drive and build quality. We agree the Era and other vans with the same layout are out because we'd have to make the bed every night.

Not far from Winnebago, we see the Hymer/Roadtrek booth. Shortly after we discovered Hymer at the Tampa RV show, the company bought Roadtrek, and while it seems like they are keeping the two brands separate, they share a space at the show. As we approach the Hymer display, we see four of their new Aktivs on the ProMaster chassis lined up with people going through each one.

Walking towards the first one, Kait stops me and says, "We've got a meeting with Hymer on Monday. Why don't we just come back and go through it then?"

"I want to go through it without the people from Hymer around to see if it's still something we're interested in. If we don't like it, no reason to sit down and talk to them."

"Good point," Kait says. "You lead the way."

Walking up to the Aktiv, the large sliding door is open, and Leo jumps right in, laying down behind the driver's seat that's been flipped around to face a fold-out table. Stepping inside, I sit down in the passenger seat which is also flipped around. I'm impressed with how open this space feels and love the sunlight coming in from the large skylight above me. The rear door of the Aktiv suddenly opens, and Kait steps up onto the rear of the van and asks, "Are you able to put the bed down?"

The bed in the Aktiv is in three parts. The center section is able to be raised and locked into place, allowing someone to walk through the van, store bikes, kayaks or anything else you may need extra room for. After closing the sliding door so Leo doesn't run off, I lower the platform for the bed and Kait helps me arrange the cushions. We jump onto the bed, lying down to see if we fit. The mattress is firm for my taste but Kait likes it. At just over nineteen feet, the Hymer is the shortest van we're considering and we'd have to sleep side to side rather than front to back. The bed is just long enough that my feet don't hit the wall. My only concern would be that one of us would have to climb over the other if that person wanted to go to the bathroom in the middle of the night.

After a few minutes of laying there, getting a feel for the bed, we move into the front living room and sit down across from each other. We open the window and sliding door which provides a lot of airflow. Leo seems comfortable in his spot under the steering wheel. The chairs and table seem to be set up nicely so that we could work in the space and have people over.

We sit there for the next fifteen minutes pretending to work, watch TV and a variety of other day-to-day activities. Kait makes a mock meal, and I pretend to use the bathroom. The bathroom is definitely tight and it would be tough to take a shower in there, but as Kait suggested, we can shower at campgrounds or the gym.

Looking around, Kait asks, "Do you think there is enough room in here for Leo?"

"Absolutely. He'd love that area under the bed. I feel like that would become his den. Plus I was reading that you can run the AC off the battery system in here. If the batteries drain below a certain point, the engine will turn on and charge them back up using a second alternator and then turn off after thirty-five minutes."

"That would be great. Just pop the AC on for the little guy and we wouldn't have to worry," Kait says. "I'm definitely interested in sitting down to talk to Susan on Monday."

"So am I. Why don't we do a quick lap around the show and then head back to the motorhome?"

On our quick tour of the grounds, we spot a few more Class B RVs that we like and make notes of what we plan to explore tomorrow. We get recognized—I should say Leo gets recognized—a few times as we're walking through the show, and, as always, he's a hit with the crowd. It's a bit weird getting recognized by people because they know all about us but we know nothing about them. At the same time, it's very uplifting because many of the people we meet tell us how much our videos have helped them in various ways and it motivates us to continue creating content.

We're up early for day two of the show. The weather report is warning us that the temperatures today will be nudging past 100, so we want to get to the show while it's still cool and before the Saturday crowds arrive. As Kait's packing up our gear, I take Leo for a walk around Prado Park. Leo is particularly interested in the different birds that are floating in the small lake, so we walk by there during our loop. I swear, if I didn't have him on a leash, he'd probably shed any fear he has of water and go in after one of those birds.

Back at the motorhome, Leo refuses to go inside. He knows we're leaving and is dragging me towards the Jeep. As much as we'd love to take him, it's going to be way too hot. While he might enjoy the hot, dry weather, I don't think he'd like walking around on that burning blacktop all day. One trick that always works when he's acting up is to just take him for another long walk, and that's exactly what I do. By the time we're finished with our second loop, he's excited to go back inside. Although it's only eight in the morning, it's already pushing past eighty out there.

When we arrive at the show, the first RVs we want to see are Leisure Travel Vans (LTV). Although they're bigger than what we've been looking for, Kait popped her head in yesterday and really liked what she saw. Walking towards the booth, a gentleman and his wife stop us. They've been watching our videos for a few months and stopped to tell us that we were the ones who inspired them to retire a bit early and get on the road.

"That's awesome!" Kait exclaims. "Which RV do you have?"

"Leisure Travel," the gentleman says, pointing towards their booth. "We were just over there talking to Dean and then saw you two, so we thought we'd say hello. If you'd like, I can introduce you to him. He's a bit of an internet sensation too; you'll really like him."

"That'd be great, thank you," Kait says.

A few minutes later, we're introduced to Dean, and I can see why so many people like him. He has a great personality and makes you feel very comfortable. After chatting for a couple minutes, Kait asks if he can show us through their different models. The first one we walk into is the Unity, and as he begins showing us the features, Kait stops him, "Dean, do you mind if we film this?"

"Not at all, film away."

The next fifteen minutes are a blur. Dean moves through each one of their models like a magician. One minute we were looking at two chairs and a table, the next he transforms the area into a bedroom. We were amazed at how much thought has gone into the designs of the different models. Unfortunately LTV no longer makes a traditional Class B camper van and are focused on the small Class C motorhomes. These are bigger than what we're looking for, but we're very impressed with their models.

"All of the models I've shown you so far are on the Mercedes chassis, but I want to show you our latest model, the Wonder, on the Ford Transit diesel chassis," Dean says.

As we step in, Dean manipulates a few things and brings down a Murphy bed which lays down over the couch in the living room. "I love it!" Kait exclaims. "This is brilliant, you can keep the bed made and it doesn't interfere with anything during the day when you put it away."

Dean continues showing Kait through the Wonder while I film. He shows her the full bathroom in the rear, closet, large kitchen and all of the storage. Stepping outside, Dean walks her through all of the outdoor storage, and I can tell she's in love.

"Dean," I say, getting his attention. "What's the towing capacity on this?"

"The Wonder comes standard with a 3,000 pound hitch receiver with wiring."

After a number of questions from Kait, we finally say our goodbyes to Dean and continue strolling through the show.

"Honey, I loved the Wonder," Kait says "I mean, that Murphy bed would be perfect for us."

"It was really nice, but it's a lot bigger than what we're looking for. Remember, our big requirement was that whatever we get has to fit in a standard parking spot because we don't want to have to tow the Jeep with us. The Wonder is over twenty-four feet long which means we'd want to bring the Jeep. Problem is that it only has a 3,000 pound tow hitch which isn't enough to tow the Jeep. If we bought that, we'd have to sell the Jeep and buy something else."

"Well, let's see what else we find. I definitely want to put the Wonder on our list of possibilities," Kait responds. Although the Wonder falls short of our main must have, I can tell she loves it.

Monday, October 10th, 2016

"Wakey, wakey, eggs and bakey," I say standing over Kait. Opening her eyes, she looks up at me as I say, "Happy Birthday!"

With a big smile on her face, she yawns and says, "Thank you, honey. What time is it?"

"Just after nine. I was excited about our meeting today and woke up early. I have something for you," I say opening the closet behind me and turning around with my hands cupped.

"I told you not to get me anything!"

"Damn!" I exclaim with a sly smile. "You guessed what it is!"

I open my hands to reveal they're empty. "Got you!"

"I really thought you got me something," Kait says laughing. "I better get up if we're going to get to the show on time."

We get to the show twenty minutes before our meeting and head straight to the Hymer booth. Upon arriving, we take a look through some of the Roadtreks on display. We like a few of the different models, but the Aktiv is still our favorite.

"Hi, are you Susan?" Kait asks as we approach a woman who looks like the person we're supposed to meet.

"Yes, Joe and Kait?" She asks.

"That's us, so great to finally meet," Kait responds.

"I was going to say the same thing," Susan says. "I feel like I already know you two from your videos. Where's Leo?"

"It's way too hot out here for him," I say. "He's much happier sleeping in the motorhome with the AC on. It's supposed to be cooler tomorrow, and we were going to bring him over, so if you're here, we can swing by again."

"Absolutely, I'd love to meet him!"

Since it is so hot, Susan suggests we commandeer an Aktiv to use as a meeting space. They have the AC running in all of them so we happily agree. Susan tells us that she really enjoyed the videos we produced at the Tampa show, has been following us ever since and would like the opportunity to work with us.

"What did you have in mind?" I ask.

"I know you already have an RV, but would you consider a Class B?"

Kait and I look at each other and then Susan. "We've actually been seriously thinking about moving down to a B for full-time use," I say. "We've been shopping and the Aktiv is at the top of our list."

"So you'd sell your motorhome and downsize to a van?" She asks.

"That's the plan. We'd like to have something by the end of the year." Kait says.

"Well, we're looking for a young couple to travel around in the Aktiv and show people what van life is like. If that sounds like something you'd be interested in, we'd like to put you in an Aktiv."

We spend the next half hour discussing some of the details of what our partnership with Hymer would look like and some next steps. They're proposing to give us an Aktiv to use for a year. They don't expect anything from us except to keep making the types of videos we have been. Susan explains that they really like what we do and simply want us to continue doing what we have been, but in their van. Before we commit to anything I ask Kait if she'd like to take one for a drive.

"Absolutely," Kait says.

"We have a demo unit out in the parking lot that we've been using for test drives," Susan responds. "Let me get the keys, and we can take it out."

Driving the Hymer is a lot like driving a large SUV or passenger van. It doesn't feel like an RV at all. The van handles well in corners, is smooth over bumps and the six cylinder gas engine has plenty of power. Aside from a quick drive in the Era when we were filming Big Time RV, this is the first van we've taken out for a drive.

As Kait is driving I look over from the passenger seat and ask, "What do you think?"

"I love the way it drives. This is so much easier than driving our motorhome!"

With a sarcastic tone I ask, "Excited?"

"Of course! I can't wait to move in!"

"Then I'll get you one for your birthday," I say with a smirk.

After returning the van, we head back to the motorhome to walk Leo and enjoy the rest of Kait's birthday as a family.

BONUS CONTENT: Our first walk-through of the Hymer Aktiv at the California RV Show: https://youtu.be/QCGzJ9U-G_M

25. FOR SALE

Wednesday, October 19th, 2016

"Did you see the email from Susan?" Kait yells from inside the motorhome.

Leo and I are sitting outside at our campground, enjoying the morning. He's been watching everyone walk past with their pups while I've been enjoying a cup of coffee and my book.

"No, let me check," I respond, setting the Kindle down. I pull up the email app on my phone and open Susan's email. Since the California RV show, we've traded a few emails with Susan trying to find out when we can take delivery of the Hymer. Unfortunately for us, since demand is so high, our delivery date has been pushed back a few times. Based on Kait's tone, it sounds like this latest email from Susan may have some good news.

As I finish reading, Kait walks out and sits across from me. Leo jumps up to greet her and is immediately embraced in a bear hug. "So, what do you think?" She asks, looking up from the giant fur ball.

Susan explains in her email that Hymer is coming out with a 2.0 model of the Aktiv which is about a foot longer. The floorplan is exactly the same, except the bed will be longer and there will be more storage in the back. It would still be short enough to fit in a standard parking spot. The downside, however, is that if we want to proceed with the 2.0, we'll have to wait an additional few months.

"I'm definitely interested," I tell Kait

"Do you think it's worth waiting for?"

"I do. I think the extra room and storage will come in handy since we'll be living in it full-time. How do you feel?"

"I'm fine either way," Kait says. "The extra room would be nice, but I know you're anxious to get the van."

"True, but, again, I think the wait would be worth having the extra space. Plus Leo will have more space under the bed. Speaking of which, where did he go?"

"Oh, he's right there," Kait says pointing behind me.

Turning around, I see Leo has somehow crawled under the motorhome. I ask him how he plans to get out, and instead of responding he rolls over and goes to sleep.

"What do you want to do for the next few months?" Kait asks.

"I don't know. We're going to need time to move out of this and get it ready to sell."

"How long do you think that will take?"

"It will depend on how we price it. Winter is not a popular buying season for motorhomes, so it may take a few months."

"I don't think it's going to take that long," Kait says, taking a pause. "Do you think we should wait to try selling the motorhome until we get the van?"

"If we wait till we get the van we'll have to stay local until the motorhome sells, and we could be stuck for a month or two waiting. On the flip side, if we put it up for sale now and it sells in a few weeks, we're going to have to figure out a place to live until we get the van."

"Our contract with Hymer is only for a year," Kait says. "I don't think the motorhome is going to take that long to sell, but regardless of how long it takes, I'd rather hit the road right after we take delivery. Plus, we'll have to store the motorhome somewhere until it sells. Do you think your mom would let us live at her house until we get the van?"

"Are you kidding? She'd love to have us."

"Then why don't we list it. Maybe we can get some 'For Sale' signs and put them in the window when we're at RV parks like this one. Good luck, honey!"

"What? You're not going to help?" I ask in a joking tone.

"Nope! You're the salesman in the family."

"True, but you're the Price Terminator."

"Yep, so you'd better not sell it too low," Kait says with a big smile, "or I'll be back".

"Well, bud," I say looking over at Leo, "why don't you and I take some pictures."

After my last sip of coffee, I go inside and grab our camera. The motorhome looks great parked at this campground, so I figure a few photos of it here will show people what it's like to be all set up and enjoying the campground.

When we first started looking for RVs, most of our searches led us to RV Trader, an online classified site for new and used RVs so I figure that's where I'll post the motorhome first. After my brief photo session, I download the photos to my laptop and start putting the ad together. We've taken great care of the motorhome, had most of the warranty work done at the factory and made a few upgrades. I list everything in the description and then get to the part where it asks how much I want to sell it for.

Looking at similar used models for sale, I'm surprised by how much they are asking. We bought ours new for

$102,000 and there are a few people trying to sell the exact same model used for more than that. The average seems to be around $100,000 so that's where I set our price. I figure it gives me room to negotiate and still make the Price Terminator happy.

Once the ad is posted, I have another idea of how we can try to sell the motorhome. "Let's make a quick YouTube video letting our audience know we're selling the motorhome," I tell Kait, as Leo and I come back inside. "We have almost 10,000 subscribers and some of them might be interested."

"That's a great idea. When do you want to shoot it?"

"Let's do it now," I suggest. "Once we publish the video, I can add a link to our RV Trader classified ad."

"Okay, but I don't want to mention anything about Hymer since we don't have a contract yet and nothing is set in stone."

"I think we tell our audience that we're still shopping. That leaves things open in case the Hymer partnership doesn't work out or we find something we like more," I tell Kait.

We set the camera up on the tripod and sit down on the couch. As we begin the video, we tell our audience about future plans and that we've decided to sell the motorhome. When we finish, I get to work on editing the video. Since it was just the two of us talking, there's little to fix and I've got something to upload an hour later. Kait and I both feel a little nervous because now that we've published the video, we've committed ourselves to this decision.

The next morning, I sit down with my laptop and start going through the comments people have left on the video. I'm not sure what I expected but they are all over the place. Some people are excited for whatever we do next. Others are upset and some think we're making a mistake. Most of those who think we're making a mistake are commenting that if we sell now, we'll be loosing 30-40% because of depreciation. While this might be true for some RVs, even if we sell ours on the lower end of what we'd want ($90,000) and include the tax we paid when we bought it plus finance charges, we'd take about a 20% loss. A 20% loss is significant but we don't think that we made a mistake. We've lived in this for almost a year and a half and we've been able to see a big part of this country. The loss we take on this, to us, is worth it for what we've been able to see and experience as a family.

As I'm going through the comments, I realize that we're not going to be able to travel. Since I've listed the motorhome for sale in the Los Angeles area, if people want to come look at it, we can't be halfway across the country. Plus, we're going to need to clean and have it ready to show which means moving most of our stuff out. After weighing our options, I sit down with Kait to discuss what I'm thinking.

"We can park the motorhome outside my mom's like we did after her surgery," I suggest. "It will be easy to move our stuff into her house and we won't have to pay to store it some place."

"What about the neighbors? When we left your mom's house last month, the tires were chalked and there was that notice we had to move the motorhome. How long do you think we can keep it there before someone calls the city again to complain?"

"Oh I forgot about that," I say with a concerned look. "You know what, I have another idea. We can get an RV spot at the Elks Lodge."

For years, a friend of mine has been trying to get me to join the Elks Lodge. Kait and I enjoyed going to their events and meeting the people there, but I was just too busy with work to participate. When I saw him last month, he suggested again that I join. He told me that the local lodge has ten RV spots with hookups and we could stay there any time we were in town for a nominal fee. Plus there are lodges across the country that we can stay at. According to him, a lot of RVers are members because of that benefit. After a bit of discussion, Kait and I decide that it's the right time to join. We both like what the organization does for the community and think it will be a great way to camp around the country. Most lodges have a bar and serve dinner, so we figure it will be fun to visit the different lodges and meet new people as we travel.

"That's a great idea plus, we can run the AC if it's hot and your mom is only a few minutes away. How long can we stay there?"

"I think they have a two-week limit, but let's first worry about joining."

"Sounds good," Kait says. "I'm excited about cleaning out the motorhome and getting rid of more stuff!"

26. DOWNSIZING...AGAIN

Thursday, October 20th, 2016

We're set to check out of the campground tomorrow and move the motorhome to my mom's house while I'm waiting to go through the process of becoming an Elk. We've agreed that while we're there, we'll get rid of everything we don't plan to take in the van. This will give us a chance to see if what we're bringing is adequate or if there are things we left behind that we need.

I'm not sure what the exact carrying capacity of the Hymer will be, but my guess is that after adjusting for the weight of a full tank of water, Kait, Leo and myself, we may have around 600 pounds of carrying capacity. It might be more than that but we won't know until we take delivery and get it weighed. It's not much considering we probably have about 1,500 pounds of stuff in the motorhome now.

Since it's hard to visualize exactly how much 600 pounds of stuff is, Kait and I decided to weigh some of the things we plan to bring which should help give us some sort of idea. The plan was that I hold bags of our things, step on the scale and write down the difference in weight between what it reads and what I weigh. Stepping on the scale to get my initial weight, the digital display reads 214.

"I need to lose some weight," I say.

"We both do, but look at it this way. The more weight we lose the more stuff we can bring," Kait says and then turns to Leo. "Don't worry, bubs, we're not putting you on a diet. You don't need to lose any weight."

Kait hands me our camera gear first. I step back on the scale. 260. "Forty-six pounds," I tell Kait who makes a note of it.

We continue this routine with our clothes, kitchen gear and other essentials. The total is 300 pounds. Considering the pile of stuff, we both feel good about the total. There's a lot more we need to bring, but at least this gives us some idea. When I express how excited I am about how much stuff we'll be able to bring along, I get a long stare from Kait with a look I know all too well.

"We have a lot of downsizing to do if we're going to live in a van," Kait says. "It's twenty feet long with limited storage. We're only going to have enough room to bring the essentials, and with all your coffee gear, there isn't going to be much room left."

She's right. I've been holding onto hope that we'd be able to bring a lot more than we probably can. Kait has a much easier time letting go of things than I do. When we were moving from the house into the motorhome, one of the hardest things for me was downsizing my tools. I left behind a lot, but this time I am only going to be able to bring a fraction of what's left. I'm beginning to wonder if this was a mistake.

"What's wrong?" Kait asks.

"Just thinking about all of the stuff I'm going to have to sell or donate and wondering if we'll be able to live in such a small space. The motorhome is about 250 square feet, and the van is going to be less than a 100 with a wet bath I can barely stand in and a four-and-a-half gallon cassette toilet."

"Listen," Kait says, "we'll have plenty of room for you to bring what you need. You know me, I don't need much which will give you more storage space. Just bring the essentials, and if you need a tool or something we don't have, ask someone to borrow it. It's certainly going to take some time to adjust to the small space, but I think we'll be fine. I've been wondering about the bathroom too and that worries me a bit. We've never used a cassette toilet, and we'll probably have to dump it every day or two. I've been reading up on them, and people say you can dump it into a standard toilet, but I don't think I could walk into a store with it and dump it into their bathroom. It's going to be one of those things we figure out on the road."

"There are just a lot of unknowns, and I'm second-guessing our decision," I tell Kait.

"We don't have to move into the van," Kait says. "The contract with Hymer isn't signed and we don't have to sell our motorhome. If this isn't something you want to do, we can say no."

"That's not it. You know me, I overthink everything and try to have it all planned out in my head. If I can't, then I start second-guessing. That's all I am doing right now. Same thing I did when we were about to sell our house and buy the motorhome. I guess we just have to take a risk and go for it, right?"

"Right, but you're still going to have to get rid of a lot of stuff," Kait says with a wink.

The next day we pull up to my mom's house after a two hour drive. While most of the country is starting to cool down, it's still in the nineties here. It cools off nicely at night

TALES FROM THE OPEN ROAD

so the motorhome will be comfortable to sleep in, but it will be nice to have my mom's house to use during the day. While Kait is helping me back the motorhome under the large tree in front of the house, my mom comes out to greet us.

"Hey, you two," she says giving us both a big hug. "Here, Joe, I thought you might want a cup," she says, handing me a fresh, piping cup of hot coffee.

"Thanks, Mom!"

When I was a kid, my parents would take my sister and me to a large farmers market that has long been a permanent fixture in L.A. Before we'd do any shopping, we'd always stop at this one place to get donuts. My parents would order three cups of coffee. One for each of them and another for me. I didn't drink it but I would use it to dip my donuts in. By the time I was finished there would be very little coffee, and my dad would usually take the last sip or two with all of the droppings and sugar from my dunked donuts.

Fast forward to my twenties and I was probably drinking a couple pots of coffee a day. After college I moved back in with my parents, and there was always a pot of hot coffee available. A fresh pot was brewed after dinner and then another before bed. If there wasn't a pot brewed, one simply had to ask if anyone else wanted any before starting a new pot, and the answer was almost always yes.

This morning when I called to tell my mom we'd get to the house by noon, she told me she'd have a fresh pot ready when we got there. This has been our family's way of welcoming someone for as long as I can remember. "Welcome, would you like a cup of coffee? I just made a fresh pot."

Taking a sip, I tell the ladies that if they take Leo in with them, I will get the motorhome settled. The first thing I do is turn the kitchen and bathroom fans on. The two fans can move quite a bit of air, and with the windows open, the motorhome stays relatively cool. Next, I plant the driver's side hydraulic jacks and then use the passenger side jacks to help stabilize us. With the crown in the road, this keeps things level and allows me to put the bedroom slide out. Since the slide's on the sidewalk side, I can extend it without worrying about blocking the road. Unfortunately, we have to leave the full-wall slide on the driver's side retracted. I'm less worried about blocking the road and more concerned about a trash or delivery truck hitting it as they drive by. Finally, I uncoil our extension cord and plug into an outlet in the garage. We can't run the AC off the standard twenty-amp household plug, but we can pretty much power everything else with no problem.

Sitting with my coffee, I have to laugh. Looking back to when we hit the road a year ago, this process would have taken the two of us twice as long as it just took me. It's just a combination of experience and familiarity. For example, it might have taken us three or four tries to get the motorhome level, whereas now I can do it in one try by myself. It's a matter of getting a feel for where to best park the motorhome (making sure it's not too off level) and whether or not you need blocks under the wheels to help keep them from coming off the ground. What was once a complicated procedure is now something quick and simple.

This is almost a metaphor for our life on the road. When we started it was tough. We missed different things about our old lives, we got on each other's nerves, and I was always stressed about whether or not we'd find a place to camp the following night. Now it's all second nature. We've learned tricks along the way to find places to camp (like being able to sleep at a Cracker Barrel) and turned our adventure into a roaming reunion with friends and family. The small community we had when we lived in L.A. has simply expanded to reach across the country and everywhere feels like home now.

Realizing all of this makes me feel a lot better about our decision to move into a van. I know there will be a lot of things to work out, but in the end we'll figure it out, and it will become just as routine as things are today. You know one other thing I've realized? I come up with some great stuff when I have a cup of coffee in my hands!

"We're all set," I announce as I come in the house and pour myself another cup.

"Did you plug us in?" Kait asks.

"I did, and I have all the fans running so it should stay cool. Where's Leo?"

"Out in the backyard. As soon as we came in, he ran straight for the fig tree."

"Of course he did. I just hope he doesn't eat too many rotten figs and make a mess later."

A few minutes later, I see Leo eyeing a large branch covered in ripe figs. He then kind of stands on his rear legs and grabs the branch in his mouth. It's gives under the pressure and he drags it to the middle of the yard where he lays down and begins feasting on the figs. "There isn't going to be a fig tree left if Leo keeps this up," I say to myself.

Saturday, October 22nd, 2016

After spending yesterday relaxing with my mom, Kait and I begin the process of downsizing our lives once again. Although we've continued to get rid of things we don't use, we can probably only bring about a quarter of what we have in the motorhome, if that. The difficult part here is we have no idea how much stuff we'll be able to bring. When we moved from the house into the motorhome, we had the motorhome parked in the driveway and knew exactly what we could bring. Now we're having to guess.

"Let's start with the bays and then move inside," I suggest.

"What are we going to do with everything?"

My mom's driveway is wide enough to park three cars so I figure we can use it to sort everything.

"Let's make three piles. We'll put our 'must haves,' over here next to the garage. To the right, put our 'maybes,' and then everything we're getting rid of will go over here next to the grass."

"Okay," Kait says with a smile. "Let's get started."

Starting at the rear of the motorhome, we open each bay, remove the contents and place them in one of the three piles. Kait is also tossing items directly into a trashcan, which magically appeared while I was pulling out all of my tools.

My plan with the tools is to sort through everything and put together a tool kit for the van. I can get rid of most of the heavy tools because I'm not planning on working on the van itself. I'll have enough to fix basic things, but if we have a major problem we'll just have to call someone or take it in. I'll keep my screwdrivers, some adjustable wrenches, pliers, wire cutters, a metric set of sockets, and, of course, a hammer and some duct tape.

Twenty minutes later Kait walks over to examine the tools I am taking. Puzzled, she asks, "Why do you need so many screwdrivers? Don't you just need the flat head and Phillips?"

"Because they're different sizes and lengths," I say, holding up two different sized Phillips screwdrivers. "I might need the short stubby one to get into a tight spot or this longer one to get those hard to reach areas. This one," I say holding up an oversized flat head, "can also be used as a wedge or small pry bar."

Kait simply shakes her head and walks back toward the motorhome. Looking back across my tools, I'm nervous about leaving so many behind because it's always the tool you don't have that you need. At the end of the day, however, I don't have room for all of them. I've realized that in adopting this small, minimalist lifestyle that I also have to adopt the mindset to go with it. Sure, I could bring more tools, but that would mean having to leave something else behind that I need. The saving grace here is that my mom has some extra space in her garage she's agreed to let us use. So while I can't bring all of my tools with me, I don't have to get rid of them.

As I am sorting items into piles, I ask myself if each item is something I really need, or is it just nice to have. I need my coffee gear, but I am letting go of my six cup Chemex. It's a tall glass coffee pot shaped like an hourglass. While it's nice to have, I can make single cups in my pour over and give the Chemex to my mom to use.

Going through my clothes, anything that is worn out or faded is put aside along with things I haven't worn. A couple sport coats and dress shoes go into the 'not bringing' pile along with more than half my clothes. What's funny is that when I first did this exercise moving from our home into the motorhome, it was much harder. Kait had to make many of the hard decisions for me, and I resented having to leave things behind. Now I'm finding it fairly easy to shed excess weight and my 'must have' pile is much smaller than I thought it would be. Kait's actually suggested that I may want to reconsider a few of the things I'm planning to get rid of.

Until you've actually gone and gotten rid of everything in your life but what's absolutely necessary (trust me, the coffee stuff is absolutely necessary), you can't imagine how cleansing it feels. I've learned through this process on multiple occasions that the more I have, the more it weighs me down.

After a few hours, we have everything out of the motorhome and my mother's driveway looks like an elaborate garage sale.

"Now what?" Kait asks.

"Let's move our 'must haves' back into the motorhome since we're going to be staying at the Elks. We can test to see if we have everything we need or if there are some items we should bring instead."

"I like that idea, but what are we going to do about all of this?" Kait asks, sweeping her hand towards everything else on the driveway.

"Let's go through everything we've decided not to bring, and if we can't sell, donate or give away an item, we throw it away. All the stuff in the 'maybe' pile can be put in trash bags and stored in my mom's house. She said we could have the guest room if we sell the motorhome before we get the van, so let's store it there for now."

"Speaking of selling the motorhome, any update?"

"I've gotten a few emails from people but no one serious yet. I'm thinking of dropping the price."

"I'm good with that. It would be nice to sell it and have one less thing to worry about."

"Agreed. Well, let's get all this stuff packed up. I'll grab the trash bags."

BONUS CONTENT: Kait managed to get me on camera going through my tools, showing what I was planning to bring (and I may have snuck a few more things into that pile): https://youtu.be/uh14_9gjyms

27. SOLD!

Wednesday, November 23rd, 2016

The last month has been stressful. Continued delays with Hymer have us second guessing if this partnership with them will ever happen. We've actually gone back to the drawing board and are looking at other possibilities. One option we're considering is a small trailer we can tow with the Jeep. We're also looking again at used Sportsmobiles.

We took a few days and traveled up to the Lance and Sportsmobile factories to film a tour of each factory and a couple of their products. We really like the Lance 1475. It would be pushing the limits of what our Jeep is capable of towing, but it's an option. At Sportsmobile (SMB), we were amazed at how customized some of their units can get. We saw one that a customer ordered for hunting trips. It had a huge bed to accommodate multiple people and a small gun safe. Another was being built for a customer who already has multiple SMBs and wanted this one outfitted with a long platform that would extend from the rear of the van. On this tray he'd mount a stationary bicycle and planned to use the van as a mobile gym. Amazing.

After the factory tours and a quick stop with Leo in Sequoia National Park, we headed back to the L.A. area and secured ourselves a site at the Elks Lodge. Kait and I have been enjoying their weekend burger cook-outs and it's nice to be able to walk in from the parking lot to have lunch.

"We just got an email from someone interested in buying the motorhome," I tell Kait.

"What did they say?" She asks.

"They want to come take a look at it Friday or Saturday and asked if we would be available."

"As long as it's not today. We promised to help your mom get ready for Thanksgiving."

Turning, I look around the motorhome and scratch my head. "There's one catch. He says his wife is very allergic to dog dander. I told him we have a dog but he doesn't think it would be a problem if we vacuum well."

"Uh, we have a lot of work to do then." Kait says in a very stressed tone. "We're going to have to detail this place so there's no hair."

Kait seems to be fully aware of the task we have ahead of us. We've always joked that wherever we take Leo, he always leaves a little bit of himself behind. The "joy" of owning a husky is that they never stop shedding. To give you an idea, in about five minutes of brushing Leo, I can fill up a plastic grocery bag full of hair. Huskies also blow their undercoat twice a year and when that happens, it looks like it's snowing. Needless to say there is white hair in every nook and cranny of this thing that we need to get out.

"If we're going to vacuum up all of his hair, we shouldn't bring Leo back in here or we're going to have to do it all over again," Kait says. "When we take him over to your mom's house for Thanksgiving, let's plan to leave him there until this is sold."

"As much as I hate to leave the little guy, my mom will love it and we can spend the day over there with him and just come back here to sleep," I say. "Oh, speaking of which, the Lodge let me extend our stay here another two weeks. The woman said the two week limit is only for visiting members and we can stay as long as we want. They don't want us living here full-time, but they said we can keep the motorhome here until we sell it."

"Oh, great. Let's hope it doesn't take much longer to sell. Speaking of which, if it doesn't sell, would you be open to renting it? There are services that will rent it for us and they cover things like insurance and that."

Sitting on the couch, I think for a moment before responding. "I've thought about that, but I don't think it would work for us."

"Why not?"

"Well, we'd still have to store the motorhome someplace and take care of it between rentals. There's maintenance and damage to deal with, plus I think we'd have to be available when people come to pick it up to show them how to use everything. I don't know how we'd do that when we're traveling full-time. Honestly, even if we could manage it, it would be nice to have one less thing to worry about while we're on the road. Same reason we decided to sell the house and not rent it."

Thursday, November 24th, 2016

Since we spent most of yesterday helping my mom get ready for Thanksgiving, Kait and I are both up and cleaning the motorhome by 7:30 a.m. On our way back from my mom's house last night, we picked up a large air purifier that we plan to leave running in the motorhome while we're gone today. While Kait's cleaning, I take another couple boxes of stuff over to my mom's house for storage, and by 11:30 we're done and ready to relax with family.

We missed Thanksgiving with family last year, opting instead to spend it on the road at the campground in Texas. The event was fun, but nothing like being with close family and friends, enjoying a home-cooked feast. My mom roasted a turkey yesterday for gravy and leftovers for people to take home and another turkey for the meal. I grilled one (it came out a bit overdone), but people didn't seem to mind because of how much other food we had. Stuffing, gravy, green beans, persimmon salad, cranberry dressing, Brussels sprouts and sweet potatoes were just about all we could fit on the table. Once dinner was done, the desserts rolled out: homemade cheesecake, pumpkin pie and Texas sheet cake all served with multiple pots of coffee.

By the time we made it back to the motorhome that evening, the air purifier had been running almost a full day and there was a noticeable difference inside. The air just smelled...cleaner. According to the prospective buyer, he and his wife planned to come by around one in the afternoon tomorrow.

When we woke up the next morning, we had an email waiting for us.

Sorry Joe, decided to go in a different direction.
Thanks,
Chuck

Tuesday, December 6th, 2016

After a month of trying to sell the motorhome, we haven't had a single person come look at it. Everyone who called or emailed saying they wanted to see it never showed. Last week Kait suggested that I contact the dealer we bought the motorhome from to see if he would be interested in buying it. Ron from the dealership got back to me and gave us two options. He'd buy it from us for $82,000 or take it on consignment and we'd net $91,000, if it sold.

After some discussion, Kait and I decided it would be better to have him take it on consignment. I'd already dropped the price to $95,000, so we figured that we'd probably make more going with Ron than if someone tried negotiating with us. Plus, he already has people coming to see Newmars so we figured he'd have an easier time selling it than we would. It seems the problem we are having is that most people don't feel comfortable buying a big-ticket item like this from a private party, preferring to go through a dealer.

"Ready to get going?" Kait asks.

In preparation to drop the motorhome off at the dealer, we emptied everything out of it and did our best to clean it from top to bottom. Ron told us not to worry about cleaning it any more as he'll have it detailed at the lot.

"Yep, I'll drive the motorhome and you follow in the Jeep."

It's cold this morning and I didn't bring a jacket, so I turn the heat on as soon as I get the motorhome started. The blower is making a strange noise that gets worse the further I drive. As soon as I turn onto the freeway, the blower stops.

"Damn," I say to myself. I try turning the heat on and off, but the blower for the dash air has completely stopped working, and we're out of warranty. Picking up the walkie-talkie, I call Kait.

"The blower for the dash air just stopped working. Can you call Newmar? We told them we were getting funny sounds from it when we were there for services but they said it was normal. Over."

"That's not good. Okay, I'll call them. Over."

By the time we get to the dealership, Kait's spoken with Newmar and they told her they would look into it and get back to us. Since we listed it as an issue during our warranty period, they should cover the repair.

"Joe, Kait, good to see you guys again," Ron says as we walk into his office.

"Hey, Ron, good to see you too," Kait replies.

"Ready to sell your motorhome? I remember you said you were only going to do this for a year. How long has it been now?"

"About a year-and-a-half," I say. "We've had a great time and are going to be sorry to see the motorhome go, but we are staying on the road. We're looking at moving down to a Class B van."

"Wow, that's quite the change. Most of my customers go bigger, not the other way around. Well, let's sit down and we can go through the consignment paperwork," Ron says, gesturing to the chairs.

"Before we get started, we had a problem with the motorhome this morning on the way here," I tell Ron.

"Let me guess, the blower motor went out?" He says with a smile. "Don't worry, Newmar already called us and is sending a part. We'll get it taken care of."

The paperwork is already on Ron's desk, and he goes through the details of the consignment. He is taking care of the detailing, marketing and selling of our motorhome. We have to keep insurance on the motorhome until it's sold. If he sells it, he'll cut us a check for the amount we agreed to, and if he hasn't sold it after three months, we will discuss what to do next.

"So, what's been your favorite place so far?" Ron asks after we sign all of the paperwork.

Kait and I look at each other and smile. Everyone we meet asks the same question and our response is always the same. "Flagstaff."

Thursday, December 8th, 2016

"Congratulations, honey," Kait says. "The numbers for November are in and we hit our goal."

Looking up from my book, I turn to Kait and ask, "We covered our monthly expenses?"

"Yep. Between our website, YouTube channel and affiliate links, we not only covered our expenses but we put some money back in the bank," she answers with a big smile.

"That's awesome! I can't believe that last December when we started producing videos we went from making $49 a month to over $3,000. If we can keep this up, we might be able to stay on the road indefinitely."

"It's taken a lot of hard work to get here but we did it," Kait says.

"Yes, we did," I say. "I also have some news for you. You know that book I've been trying to write about our adventures on the road? I've decided that while waiting to take delivery of the van, I'm going to use this time to get the book written."

"I know you can get it done, and I'm here to help if you need anything," Kait says.

For the past couple months, I've tried writing a book about what it took for us to quit our jobs and get on the road. The problem is that I can never get past the first page or two, so I've enlisted the help of someone who knows what they're doing. Kevin Tumlinson had us on his Wordslinger Podcast last year to talk about what it's like living and working on the road as he's a fellow RVer and follower of our YouTube channel. When I mentioned on his show that I had contemplated writing a book, he offered to help mentor me through the process when I was ready. So I've decided to take him up on his offer. We have a call scheduled to go over the writing process, and he said he has a few tricks to help me get started.

While we waited for the motorhome to sell, Kait and I decided to go on an actual tent camping trip. Neither of us had been tent camping in over a decade so we packed up the Jeep, grabbed Leo and headed out to Joshua Tree National Park for a few days. Since it had been so cold, we grabbed plenty of firewood and our heavy jackets. Once we arrived, we got a camp site at Jumbo Rocks and were actually quite surprised at the number of people camped at the park for a Monday.

We were both happy to be back out in the wild. We hadn't been out of the motorhome for long, but all of us, including Leo were getting a bit stir crazy staying at my mom's house. That said, I did remember why it had been so long since I'd last camped...I've never been comfortable sleeping on the ground. It reiterated why I enjoyed coming to places like this in a motorhome and I became even more excited about our upcoming van life. Our Class A never would have fit in the spots here, and we've seen quite a few different vans camped around us. We both said that once we get the Hymer, we'd like to come back out here and enjoy it with the comforts of a Class B RV.

Saturday, January 14th, 2017

After a decent writing session, I check our email and open one that Kait and I have been eagerly anticipating.

"It's sold!" I yell.

"What's sold?" Comes a chorus from my mother, aunt and Kait who are in the living room watching Jeopardy! together.

"The motorhome."

"Yay! That's great news!" They respond in unison.

Kait comes running in to where I'm working and says, "Are you serious? Our motorhome is sold? You're not messing with me?"

"Nope, Ron just emailed to let us know it's sold and we can come pick up our check," I say with a big smile.

"What a huge relief! I've been worried it wouldn't sell."

"Me too. I just hope we get the van soon. I'm ready to get back on the road."

AFTERWARD

Thank you so much for reading <u>Tales From the Open Road!</u> If you enjoyed the book, I'd really appreciate it if you can leave a review. This helps in many ways because the more reviews a book has, the more discoverable it becomes. If you didn't enjoy it, please send me a note and let me know why. I'd appreciate the feedback. Just head to our website, weretherussos.com and leave a comment anywhere on the site. Thank you.

While this book is finished, the story isn't over! The next book will be all about van life and our experiences of living full-time in a van. It was certainly an adjustment coming from our Class A motorhome.

Some of you might be wondering how I remembered so much, the conversations we had, etc. Well, I tend to remember those types of things but my biggest help were Kait's daily notes. She takes notes every day about where we went, what we ate, how we were feeling, the weather, etc. Writing this book was a fun look back in time and I can't wait to get started on the next one.

The idea to write this series started because we are always asked why we decided to live this life. The next question was always, how are we able to manage it. There's a common presumption that we must be independently wealthy in order to live life on the road, but as you saw in this book, we only had so much savings. We learned how to stretch that money, but at the end of the day, we had to figure out a way to make a living and support ourselves if we wanted to continue. Our goal with these books and the other content we produce is to inspire you to live the life you want and show you that not only is it possible, but it's sustainable. Even if you're already living your dream, we hope you got something out of these books.

To follow along on our adventures and connect with us:
Website: weretherussos.com
YouTube: youtube.com/weretherussos
Facebook: facebook.com/weretherussos
Instagram: instagram.com/weretherussos

To find out more about some of the products we use and mention in the book, head over to our store: weretherussos.com/our-store

Thank you!
Joe Russo
We're the Russos

SPECIAL THANKS

I want to say a big thank you to the following people for helping make this book a reality.

My beta readers - you did me a tremendous service and I so appreciate the feedback and notes you gave me on this book.

Todd Reimer
Gregory Yager
Kay Griffin
Mark Dyason
Mary Tsang
Shannon Hill Zuercher
Randy Andersson
And Laurie Sundbo-Sather

Our WTR Family over on Patreon - the support you've shown us not only with this book but with everything we're doing is a big motivation for us.

Our subscribers - you've kept me honest and helped push me to get this book written. I don't know how many times we've run into some of you and been asked, "Hey Joe, when's your next book coming out?"

Finally, to one of our biggest fans and supporters, Rob Abrams. You've been there since the beginning and it's been awesome having you along with us for this journey. Enjoy the paperback ;)

Thank you!!!

Made in the USA
Columbia, SC
27 December 2020